Learning Process Skills

Stanley R.

Academic Therapy Publications
Novato, California

```
LC 4704 .R54x 1992
Riley, Stanley R.
Learning process skills
       287028
```

Copyright ©1992, by Stanley R. Riley, PhD. All rights reserved. Printed in the United States of America. No part of this publication may be reproduced, stored in a retrieval system, or transmitted, in any form or by any means, electronic, mechanical photocopying, recording, or otherwise, without the prior written permission of the publisher.

Academic Therapy Publications
20 Commercial Boulevard
Novato, California 94949-6191

International Standard Book Number: 0-87879-938-9

10 9 8 7 6 5 4 3 2
0 9 8 7 6 5 4 3 2 1

TABLE OF CONTENTS

Foreword		v
Introduction		ix
Chapter I	**Learning Processes**	11
Chapter II	**Visual Processing**	19
	A. Sequencing	22
	B. Memory	27
	C. Abstraction	33
	D. Discrimination	38
	Figure-Ground	39
	Perceptual Constancy	43
	Blending & Segmenting	47
Chapter III	**Auditory Processing**	51
	A. Sequencing	54
	B. Memory	58
	C. Abstraction	62
	D. Discrimination	66
Chapter IV	**Verbal Processing**	71
	A. Production	74
	B. Response	78
Chapter V	**Kinesthetic Processing**	83
	A. Perception	86
	B. Coordination	90
	C. Learning	94
	D. Memory	98
Chapter VI	**Abstract Processing**	103
	A. Integration	106
	B. Non Verbal Concepts	110
	C. Concentration	114
Chapter VII	**Remediations**	119
	A. Remediation Plans	121
	B. Summary	123
Bibliography		125
Preliminary Evaluation		133
Verification		135

FOREWORD

The human brain is truly a remarkable and complex organ. Although great progress has been made in the analysis of neural functioning, mapping specialized areas and relating intellectual, sensory and neuro-muscular activity, precise knowledge of the memory thinking process is still in an early exploration stage. However, from what is presently known some useful generalizations can be made.

1) There is an infinite variety of basic learning process skills that must be mastered. Starting with an infant's early thinking processes and continuing throughout his life. These processes constantly evolve and change, forming a complex collection of learning skills that must be thought of as totally interdependent and impossible to separate. A lack of a specific process or a failure to learn a specific process in this complex fabric of basic learning processes results in a deficit in the child's potential for acquiring knowledge.

2) Learning is unique for each individual. Learning styles, strengths and weaknesses differ enormously from person to person. A learning style that works well for one person may be completely inadequate for another. Most teachers, even after a few days contact with school children, realize the principle of individual differences is both absolute and inescapable. Just as no two peas in a pod are exactly the same, or no two snowflakes the same, it is unreasonable to expect any two children to have any more than a superficial resemblance to one another. Students come in all sizes, shapes, colors, dispositions, interests and abilities. The idea that kids are kids and can be treated alike simply fails to take into account the unique properties of each human being. With such a diversity of raw material schools cannot be expected to turn out a uniform product.

3) Learning is a lifelong process. It begins even before birth and continues throughout life ending only with death. It is an infinitely complex series of functions, each one leading to the next, from the simplest to the most sophisticated. The steps in learning can be thought of as building blocks in a pyramid, each resting, supporting, depending on one another forming an entire structure. No single part of the structure is more important than any other part and all parts are necessary for the integrity of the whole.

4) Learning does not proceed as a continuous, orderly process. Learning does not consist of ponderous, plodding steps infinitely repeated to reach a goal. Learning is, rather, an intermittent process that goes by fits and starts with many rests and side excursions. Skill increases rise suddenly to new plateaus and remain at that level for unpredictable periods, to rise again, sometimes without practice. This time frame seems to depend upon an integrative process that takes longer for some children than others but is essential to mastery.

5) The only tool available to teachers and to most other behavioral scientists is meticulous observation and analysis of the end result of intellectual activity: The behavior of the subject. Using this tool, inferences and deductions may be postulated concerning the presence, proficiency and efficiency of the intellectual process. Direct cerebral intervention is beyond the present scope of the educational process, information cannot be placed in the brain by physical means. However, as a student engages in carefully selected activities and a change in the end behavior is observed, then a change in the pattern of intellectual processing has probably occurred.

Undoubtably, there are kinds of learning problems that do not fit the modalities and their component processes presented in this work. The modalities presented here can serve as an adequate basis for dealing with many of the problems that are faced in the classroom. They can be profitably used as workable principles for determining probable causes of learning problems and helpful in the selection of suitable, effective remedial activities.

Any evaluation of an individual's educational ability is a very complex process. The opportunity for error is great and considerable care should be exercised by the individual charged with the responsibility of making critical observations for predictive purposes.

An observation of this sort should include a lengthy personal observation by someone who is eminently qualified through thorough training and experience. It should also include several objective test scores in the specific areas being evaluated. One test score is like one musical note, it is meaningless by itself. Place the same note with other notes arranged by an individual who is qualified through thorough training and experience and the result can be beautiful and possess significant meaning. So it is with test scores. When they are combined with personal observation and arrangement by a qualified person they can be of enormous significance in the educational life of the individual being evaluated.

Included in this text are instructions for personal observation techniques for each learning process skill. Also included are lists of commonly used tests that can be used in addition to the personal observations to verify and substantiate a specific diagnosis. These lists will be found in the appendix.

INTRODUCTION

Each year, opening day of school is an exciting, exhilarating experience. The happy, smiling faces of the children as they troop in from the playground, the eager, enthusiastic attitude they display and the satisfied smiles of the parents and teachers on that day all combine to produce a truly pleasant experience for all involved. Young children seem especially excited by all the events of that day. Like young children everywhere, their happiness is infectious.

By the time these same children reach the upper levels of high school several years later, many of the formerly eager, enthusiastic children are bored, resentful and actively resisting the educational process. Many are functionally illiterate and others can read only minimally. After many years of education, the major lessons learned are those of avoidance and failure. Even those who did not drop out but silently struggled through to their diploma consider what occurred in the classroom as totally unrelated to real life.

Yet learning is as natural as breathing. A child's whole life is filled with learning. Enormous amounts of new data fill their every waking moment. Some social scientists have suggested that by the time a child begins formal schooling he has accumulated more information than he will learn in the rest of his life.

Very young children are infinitely curious. They will watch a crawling bug for a very long time. They are curious about almost every aspect of that bug, including sadly, what happens when it is smashed.

This curiosity is one of the strongest motivators of learning. How does it happen that this absorbing curiosity, this vital interest in all things, is almost totally absent for many students when formal education draws to a close?

There is, of course, no single answer to this question. There are many answers and it is likely the question will never be completely answered. However, one of the reasons for this strange turn of events may be that many of these turned off students simply do not have the basic equipment that is needed to learn. Somehow, one or more very basic skills have not happened for them. These basic skills and their remediation are the substance of this text.

This book is written for classroom teachers. It is designed to help upgrade teaching skills and make students more successful. Its purpose is not to provide a "cookbook" approach but, rather to provide a systematic process of attacking the learning problems of children. It is written to help teachers gain a better understanding of children who are failing in school through no fault of their own.

CHAPTER I

LEARNING PROCESSES

Some students fail to master a basic skill when it is presented in the curriculum sequence. When this happens the foundation for a serious learning process weakness has been created which, in time, tends to become fixed. Unless recognized, unlearned and retaught early in the child's school career, the resulting learning process error is often not remediable. By this means, learning process weakness is built into the student.

Learning Process Skills are those thinking patterns which must be mastered before a student can begin to perform even the simplest learning tasks. Some of these skills are learned in infancy and early childhood, some in elementary school and a few in secondary school. Unless a student can master the ability to make visual judgements and to recognize the special characteristics, similarities and differences in things he sees, he may have a great deal of difficulty learning the individual letters of the alphabet or the differences between d and b or p and q. Reading words and completing textbook or reference assignments would be an impossible task for such a student later in his career.

There is considerable evidence that learning process skills are one component of children's developmental patterns that start from modest but important early beginnings and follow a course of well defined, regular milestones. Lapses, distortions or interruptions are reflected in the child's learning behavior.

Each infant develops a unique way of sensorially interacting with his environment by his organization of the stimuli selection process. This selection process becomes an automatic or a semi-automatic process that operates below or at the threshold of consciousness. It has an important influence on the development of learning process skills.

Although there are areas that have been identified as having specialized functions such as sight and hearing, selected sensory input is processed by all areas almost simultaneously as the result of reticular systems that provide information simultaneously to many cortical areas, allowing inter-area interaction that result in meaningful gestalts. Thus, learning process skills are intellectual operations not only in the primary area of sensory input, but also almost simultaneously in many other cortical areas.

Before the simplest task of learning to read, write or do arithmetic can be performed, the mind must develop some very specific ways of regarding the environment. It must develop some specific learning process skills. For example: Before a child can understand the symbol "A" stands for the idea "A", he must have already developed a way of regarding lines and spaces and their inter-relationships. This allows the child to understand that the line"/" and the line "\" combined with the line "-" is an A and has a particular meaning. To do this, the learning process skills of Visual Discrimination, Visual Sequencing, Visual Abstraction and Visual Memory must be developed adequately or the child cannot begin to identify an "A" or understand what an "A" is all about, much less the alphabet, written words or sentences.

For the purposes of illustration and discussion, learning process skills can be conveniently grouped into five general areas necessary for academic achievement:
1. Seeing selectively.
2. Hearing accurately.
3. Reading and understanding words.
4. Coordinating visual-motor activities.
5. Thinking logically.

When a student achieves proficiency in these basic learning process skills, he can then be expected to be able to learn the basic tasks of communicative reading, writing and quantitative processing. Deficiency or weakness in any one skill or combination of skills can seriously impair the learning process.

BASIC LEARNING PROCESSES

The first category of learning process skills, seeing selectively (Visual Processing) includes six learning process skills:
1. Visual Sequencing: Perceiving logical visual sequences.
2. Visual Memory: Retrieving visual patterns.
3. Visual Abstraction: Synthesizing visual patterns.
4. Figure-Ground: Discriminating figures.
5. Perceptual Constancy: Perceiving Constancy.
6. Blending and Segmenting: Perceiving letter combinations.

The second category of learning process skills, hearing accurately (Auditory Processing) includes four learning process skills:
1. Auditory Sequencing: Retrieving auditory sequences.
2. Auditory Memory: Retrieving auditory information.
3. Auditory Abstraction: Understanding auditory information.
4. Auditory Discrimination: Hearing auditory differences.

The third category of learning process skills, speaking or reading aloud (Verbal Processing) includes two learning process skills:
1. Verbal Production: Knowledge of words.
2. Verbal Response: Using words.

The fourth category of learning process skills, coordinating visual-motor activity (Kinesthetic Processing) includes four learning process skills:
1. Kinesthetic Perception: Visual-motor discrimination.
2. Kinesthetic Coordination: Visual-motor dexterity.
3. Kinesthetic Learning: Learning visual-motor activities.
4. Kinesthetic Memory: Retaining visual-motor activities.

The fifth category of learning process skills, thinking logically (Abstraction) includes three learning process skills:
1. Integration: Using modality combinations.
2. Non Verbal Concepts: Concepts without verbalization.
3. Concentration: Focusing attention on specific stimuli

BASIC LEARNING PROCESSES

VISUAL PROCESSING
- Visual Sequencing
- Visual Memory
  - Immediate
  - Short Term
  - Long Term
- Visual Abstraction
- Visual Discrimination
  - Figure-Ground
  - Perceptual Constancy
  - Blending or Segmenting

AUDITORY PROCESSING
- Auditory Sequencing
- Auditory Memory
  - Short Term
  - Long Term
- Auditory Abstraction
- Auditory Discrimination
  - Frequency
  - Intonation
  - Intensity

VERBAL PROCESSING
- Verbal Production
  - Sounds
  - Word Concepts
  - Language Formation
- Verbal Response
  - Visual Cues
  - Auditory Cues
  - Other Cues

KINESTHETIC PROCESSING
- Kinesthetic Perception
  - Laterality-Directionality
  - Discrimination
  - Spatial Judgement
- Kinesthetic Co-ordination
- Kinesthetic Learning
  - Recall
  - Retention

ABSTRACT PROCESSING
- Integrative Learning
- Non Verbal Concept Formation
- Concentration

Although here and throughout this text each skill is presented as having a distinct and separate reality, the presentation is only for clarity and convenience of discussion. The learning process skills presented here are interdependent and interacting. The skills which are discussed in this manual are not all the skills that exist. Without doubt there are many more, some vaguely suspected, some obvious but not currently measurable and others totally unknown. The learning process skills presented here are those which are evident and currently measurable.

CHAPTER II

VISUAL PROCESSING

CHILDREN WITH VISUAL PROCESSING PROBLEMS

o Mary has a very short attention span for her age and when reading often skips words, repeats herself, cannot remember the sequence of picture stories and has difficulty making sense of most sentences she reads.

o Derek, an outgoing, pleasant child until the fifth grade, pesters his teacher about material already written on the chalkboard or in the book, copies printed problems in error and is unable to recall more than the simplest written or printed facts.

o Eight year old Sandra, usually an even-tempered, smiling, talkative girl, is easily frustrated in the classroom, has little tolerance for reading tasks and compensates by being overbearing with other children.

o Fifth grade Roger is anything but neat, can never seem to find anything, forgets what he is supposed to do and does poorly in written work although he does well in oral spelling.

All of these problems are examples of children with visual processing problems. These problems can be, for the purpose of illustration and discussion, generally divided into four groups. They will be described in the following order:

1. Sequencing.
2. Memory.
3. Abstraction.
4. Discrimination.

These groups are, of course, interdependent and interacting and the separation is academic, intended only for illustration. Thus, when a child's symptoms seem to suggest difficulties in one area, be sure to check for symptoms in other related areas.

VISUAL SEQUENCING PROBLEMS

> What they are: Visual Sequencing problems are failures to perceive and understand logical visual sequences. Children with this problem are often unable to:
> 1. Understand letters or numbers in a series.
> 2. Read and write from left to right.
> 3. Read from top to bottom.

How Visual Sequencing Works

An orderly program of eye movements must be so mastered that it becomes automatic if tasks such as reading, spelling, copying and arithmetic are to take place. This program, called Visual Sequencing, consists of three steps:
1. Left to right eye movements, with pauses along each line while information is received.
2. Return sweep movements in which the eyes move left and downward at the end of each line.
3. Wide enough visual span so that concentration on pertinent information is possible.

A fairly large number of children have difficulty developing this skill, but only a few difficulties are caused by muscular dysfunction or other physiological problems. These should be ruled out first. Most problems involve difficulties in processing information rather than difficulties in transmitting it through the optic nerves to the brain.

SYMPTOMS OF VISUAL SEQUENCING PROBLEMS

Appearance of carelessness, laziness or indifference

These qualities are often attributed to children with visual sequencing problems. The tip-off is when children continue to fail yet sincerely profess that they really have tried their best.

Tension signs

Children with problems in this area exhibit a high level of tension in the body, hands, arm, and face when performing in this area.

Guessing at material

When new information is received in garbled or fragmented form, because of failure to follow the orderly sequence, it may result in the student's guessing wildly at the meaning of the material. Some of the most humorous examples of student "goofs" that every teacher collects are the result of these wild guesses.

Reading errors

These children skip words or read parts of sentences out of order or reread parts of the same sentence. They often jump lines even when using a pointer. Their return sweep is often incomplete or jerky. They fixate or pause during the return, often landing on the wrong line either up or down. They often make long pauses between words, attacking each word as if it were a separate task, thus only "naming" words. They have difficulty in simple phrasing and trouble reading a sentence, however short, as a single idea. Although their knowledge of phonics may be good, and they may have a fairly good reading vocabulary, they take a long time completing the material. Generally their comprehension is relatively poor and fragmentary.

Spelling errors

Spelling involves the skill of being able to understand the logic of the sequencing itself. For instance: Understanding that the sequence of the letters **t - h - e** form the word "the". After one learns the mechanical task of forming the individual letters, visual sequencing is vital in learning to spell.

Copying errors

In copying, whether from a chalkboard or from a book or paper, a left-to-right pattern of eye movements is essential, both for receiving information and for transcribing it to writing. Weakness in visual sequencing may produce letter reversals, b for d, p for q. Students may also omit some parts of the material they are copying and repeat others.

Writing errors

Compositions may appear to lack simple logic, even though grammar, spelling and form may be acceptable. Students are unaware of their inability to complete a logical, coherent piece of work.

Arithmetic errors

Arithmetic requires a highly disciplined program of eye/hand movements. And, if the eyes don't track, the pencil won't either. Unless the student can find the proper place and right sequence, there will be many conclusion errors. Omissions will be common even when the child is conscientiously trying to complete the work. Assignments will be completed with little regard for sequence even when all the parts are included. Children may demonstrate a mastery of basic facts yet not be able to solve even two or three step multiplication or division problems. They will write down correct answers in the wrong places or in the wrong sequence. They almost always give the appearance of wandering through the problems blindfolded.

Simple Tests For Visual Sequencing Problems

Saying versus doing

This test is appropriate for children who are in a preschool or kindergarten reading readiness program, which is also the time when visual sequencing is very important. Have the child engage in a sequencing activity such as writing ABC's, numbers or putting colored blocks in order. If the child is able to say them in order but not write them or otherwise reproduce them in order, visual sequencing may be a problem.

Reading Aloud

If the child is able to read even a little, have the child read aloud from any book and note if any of the following occur. The child:
1. Reads one word at a time, with long pauses.
2. Jumps back over previously read words.
3. Skips one or more words while reading.
4. Seems to "name" words showing little awareness of their meaning.
5. Does not make sense of what has been read.

Charting Eye Movements

Get a blank sheet of paper and sit with the child in front of you. While the child reads, either aloud or silently, draw a picture of the child's eye movements, moving your pencil along without taking it off the paper. Don't try to be either artistic or scientifically accurate; just try to move your pencil as the child's eyes move. Make a short vertical line to represent each fixation. Make appropriate reverse lines for jumps back and appropriate advance lines for skips forward. Record all erratic eye movements - looking up, down, around, right, left, across the room and so on. Note if the child maintains his place on the line and changes to the next line without using a finger or some other sort of guide.

General Classroom Assistance

There are many things that can be done in the classroom to assist a child with this problem. Here are some examples:

1. Make assignments requiring the child's visual-sequential concentration whenever possible.
2. Place the child's seat next to the chalkboard.
3. Encourage the use of a finger or other guide to help the child maintain the place on the line and make the return sweep to the next line.
4. Have the child record all assignments and homework in detail.

Examples of Individual Remediations

The child identifies common objects and discusses details.

The game of Twenty Questions.

How to games: How to make a bed, do the dishes, etc..

Jigsaw Puzzles.

Complete simple pictures with lines missing.

Have the child describe action scenes in picture stories.

Cut out comic strips and have the child arrange in proper order.

"How to" exercises and descriptions.

Paint by number pictures.

Road map exercises: The child plans routes between points, perhaps calculating mileage.

Science experiments in which the child lists in detail the procedures, and/or observations of the experiment.

Sentence analysis involving compound sentences, complex sentences and parts of speech. This will focus attention on the whole sentence.

VISUAL MEMORY PROBLEMS

> What they are: Visual Memory problems are failures to recall what has been seen. Children with this problem are often unable to:
> 1. Recall patterns, shapes, designs or figures
> 2. Recall numbers, letters, words or phrases.
> 3. Remember details regarding what they have read or seen.

How Visual Memory Works

When visual material is perceived it is sorted, classified, arranged and stored consciously and subconsciously. Retrieval is dependent upon:

Perception

The ability to receive visual material accurately.

Concentration

The ability to focus on specific stimuli while ignoring others.

Organization

The ability to sort, classify and arrange visual material accurately and appropriately.

Experience

The unique social, emotional and cognitive background of the individual.

Recovery

The ability to recall information accurately.

Emotional Impact

The emotional impact of the material and all of the external conditions at the time of the perception are directly related to what is recalled. For example: At times when the U. S. Air Force trained its pilots in aircraft identification by using slides of various aircraft, an occasional slide showing a particularly attractive young lady would be shown to heighten interest in the slide show. Sometimes the purpose of the show was severely tested, and the pilots became more adept at young lady identification than aircraft identification.

Difference in Material

Large differences are more easily retained than small. Learning to make fine discrimination is a long and a continuous process.

Past Experience

Each new experience is immediately compared to past experiences stored in the memory. Children with limited expectations and narrow backgrounds have less background to relate to new stimuli. Their generalizations are broader, less specific and more limited than children with rich and varied experiences.

Impact of Experience

Passive experience results in much less retention that active experience. Oddly enough, incorporating activities only remotely related to the material to be learned results in greatly increased retention.

SYMPTOMS OF VISUAL MEMORY PROBLEMS

Errors in copying and transcribing

Children with difficulty in visual memory have difficulty in copying material or instructions written on the chalkboard on paper at their desks. Their visual memory is often so short that they cannot retain a word, a number or, sometimes, even a letter for the length of time it takes them to refocus their eyes or on a piece of paper at their desk. Occasionally, the slightest eye movement is so distracting that it interrupts the processing of information.

Garbled written work: skips - repeats - omissions

These students often produce garbled material leaving out essential sections and skipping about with no logical order. They cannot proof-read their own material with any accuracy because errors are invisible to them. Self correction from other material is rarely possible because content cannot be retained long enough for correction.

Poor Spelling

Because their visual memory is so poor, spelling is often a problem for these students. Written work using longer words leaves the middle somewhat jumbled with the beginning and end reasonably intact.

Reading Problems

Word guessing, substitutions of words with similar meanings, sentence condensation, omissions and flashbacks are common reading errors for children with this difficulty. These children have difficulty remembering the look or shape of a word and use the context to supply clues. There are many pauses to allow time to look back and remember.

Failure to follow written directions

Children with this problem often ask for verbal explanations from their friends or the teacher even though the written directions seem quite clear. Some will not start an assignment until they have a personal explanation of the directions. This is evidence of the child's habit of using his listening ability to reinforce his weak visual memory. It is easy to become impatient with such children. They often excuse their lack of performance by complaining that they asked the teacher for help but the teacher was too busy.

Mistakes in math problems or disordered notation

When a problem calls for more than one step, children with this problem make frequent errors in carrying on the sequence because they cannot remember what comes next. They have problems keeping columns straight in addition, bringing down the proper multipliers in multiplication and maintaining an orderly process of notation in writing down their solutions.

Poor test taking

Achievement on standardized tests is often well below the child's actual mastery of the material. They don't seem to do well and are often perceived as being careless, lazy and poorly motivated. Sometimes, a child with this difficulty can become very discouraged by the objective evidence of failure and become very emotional. This particular problem contributes to the child's feeling that the test wasn't fair or that the teacher is biased in favor of other children.

SIMPLE TESTS FOR VISUAL MEMORY PROBLEMS

Copy Words

Select a series of letters or words which seem appropriate for a particular child's age and grade level. It is good practice to give the list of words to the entire class to get a better idea of the degree of difficulty of the list and what might be average performance. Tell the children that you are going to show them some words you want them to remember. Wait until you have their attention and then display each word for a short period of time, about 15 seconds for each word. Do not show the words again and do not use the same list at a later time. After you have covered the words or placed them out of sight, have the children write them on a piece of paper. Note, if you can, children who seem to be having difficulty. Have the children turn in their papers and go on to some other aspect of the day's work. Children who perform well below average at this task probably have a visual memory problem.

Picture Recall

For students who cannot read, a similar task can be arranged using pictures instead of letters and words. Children who cannot read cannot, of course, reproduce in writing what they have seen, therefore they will have to tell what they have seen. Tape recording the entire screening will be most helpful.

General Classroom Assistance

Assignments should be recorded in a notebook to assist recall. Chalkboard assignments should be recorded in writing by the child whenever possible. Copying learning material could be helpful in retaining meanings. Auditory reinforcement of written material could be helpful to retention.

Examples of Individual Remediations

Look and Remember
a. The child looks around the room.
b. He closes his eyes and visualizes.
c. He says all the things he can remember.
d. He opens his eyes to see how right he was.

What did you see?
a. What was on the table?
b. What did you see out the window?
c. What clothes are the other people wearing?

Several objects can be displayed for about five seconds, the child closes her eyes, one object is removed and she tries to remember what it was. More objects can be added as she progresses.

The student is given a picture to look at for a short time, perhaps 15 seconds, and tries to recall the items in the picture.

A simple drawing is done on the chalkboard, the child closes his eyes and something is added, perhaps a chimney on a house. At a signal, the child opens his eyes and tries to name what has been added.

Simple geometric forms are put on flash cards and presented briefly to the child. He is then asked to reproduce them.

Cardboard geometric forms are given to the student and are traced. The child's eyes are closed and something is added. The child opens his eyes and tells what has been added.

VISUAL ABSTRACTION PROBLEMS

> What they are: Visual Abstraction problems are failures to understand the meaning of visual patterns. Children with this problem are often unable to:
> 1. Understand visual letter or word combinations.
> 2. Maintain attention to visual material.
> 3. Select significant ideas among many visual cues.

How Visual Abstraction Works

Visual Abstraction is that part of the visual process that assigns meaning to perceived patterns. It operates on two levels; conscious or subconscious and can be immediate or long term. It is dependent upon:

Perception

The ability to receive visual information accurately.

Screening

The ability to pay attention to specific stimuli while disregarding others.

Experience

New visual material is compared with previously identified patterns, past generalizations are associated and new meanings are assigned to both old and new material.

Expectation

General preparation for what is to be seen, a "mind set." New material, unfamiliar material or unexpected material may or may not be completely retained.

Organization

The ability to sort, classify, arrange and store visual information appropriately.

Retrieval

The ability to recall previously stored information accurately, appropriately and in its proper order.

SYMPTOMS OF VISUAL ABSTRACTION PROBLEMS

Distracting Behavior

The behavior of students who have problems in visual abstraction is often very annoying to teachers. Assigned a task requiring this function, the child fidgets, hums, plays with his pencil, taps his feet, talks to his neighbor and, in general, distracts his classmates. After speaking to the student several times without any apparent effect, teachers can become quite impatient.

Frequent occurrence of this type of behavior could be considered a symptom of visual abstraction problems rather than a recurring discipline problem. If the student is able to go ahead with the assigned task after a **friendly**, verbal explanation, a problem in visual abstraction could be suspected.

Work Avoidance

When the student is given an assignment sheet and he seems to be avoiding beginning the task or, cannot seem to keep on working for more than a short time without additional help, a closer look at the possible causes is indicated. Rather than face failure, some students often break their pencils, write something and then erase it, sometimes to the point of making a hole in their paper, tear up their papers and get new ones. They often never seem to accomplish anything.

Poor Production

Some students seem to working hard but an examination of their production shows they have made little progress. They often work very slowly with great deliberation that is not reflected by accuracy, parts of work may be omitted or left incomplete. Most assignments are completed in only a perfunctory manner.

Difficulty in Following Directions

Students with this difficulty have problems with following written directions, particularly when they involve a number of steps. These students often appear bewildered when faced with such a task, even when the teacher believes they are quite capable of doing the work. After some tentative starts with a little help, they do not seem to recognize the steps necessary to complete each part of the task and do not seem to be able to grasp that task as a whole. At times, steps in the directions are passed over making the following tasks impossible. Or, the task may be done out of order with disastrous results.

Violating Written Rules

Many classrooms have simple do's and don'ts posted as reminders to control routine behaviors. Many teachers feel that this is good training for the future when, as adults, they will have to obey written laws and directions. Students who protest their ignorance when they violate these written rules **may not** be doing it simply because of thoughtlessness or indifference, although this certainly could be the case. They **may** simply not comprehend the written rules because of difficulty with visual abstraction.

SIMPLE TESTS FOR VISUAL ABSTRACTION PROBLEMS

See and Tell

Present a cartoon or series of cartoons that you believe the student can identify easily. Initial success is important to gain confidence for more difficult tasks.

Say: "Tell me what is happening." If possible, tape record all answers. In any case, take notes about the items that are identified, their relationships, orderly processing, amount and richness of response and the detail reported.

Repeat, using what you think will be a more difficult set or series until the student makes obviously wrong answers or you run out of test materials.

Compare responses with children who do not seem to have the problem.

Following Written Directions

Present to the student a series of cards with carefully lettered directions. The cards should include tasks of increasing difficulty; one step tasks, then two step tasks, then three step tasks, etc.. Have the child do what the cards direct. As with the previous test, take notes carefully and compare with behaviors of children who do not have this difficulty.

General Classroom Assistance

When visual material is presented, a clear, concise, verbal explanation will be most helpful. All assignments and homework should be written in detail. Seating next to a student who can verbally explain written tasks can save much teacher time as tasks of that sort will often be confusing.

Examples of Individual Remediations

Pegboards.
Geo-boards.
Jigsaw Puzzles - appropriate for age.
Cubes with patterns.
Parquetry with patterns.
Lite-Brite. *
Part-Whole Lotto. *
Pythagoras Game. *
Word Search. *
Jumbled Sentences.
Incomplete Number Sequences.
Sentences with missing words.
Kaleidoscope Puzzles. *
Fables, appropriate for age, read and discuss.
Newspaper reports of current interest, read and discuss.

* Commercially available.

VISUAL DISCRIMINATION PROBLEMS

Visual Discrimination involves more than accurate transmission of visual stimuli to the brain. It involves a higher mental process that sorts, discards and includes available stimuli so that the transmitted image forms a "gestalt" or consistent whole.

Perceptual problems are among the more obvious causes for learning disability although they do not in themselves account for the large number of children who have learning difficulty. They are generally most obvious in children who are reported to have minimal brain dysfunction. There are many other learning problems that may be the result of neurological disturbance that do not involve visual discrimination.

The picture sent to the brain must include pertinent details and the general configuration of the bit of information perceived. The information must be accurate so that other functions can rely on the perception and perform their part of the learning process.

In general, three processes will be considered as most important in Visual Discrimination:
1. Figure-Ground Discrimination
2. Perceptual Constancy
3. Blending and Segmenting

Perceptual difficulties are seldom confined to any one of these or other processes, usually involving combinations of them. These three processes will be discussed in detail on the following pages.

FIGURE-GROUND RELATIONSHIP PROBLEMS

> What they are: Figure-Ground relationship problems are failures in the ability to see an object or objects as distinct from other objects or from the background. Children with this problem are often unable to:
> 1. Find words on a page.
> 2. Be attentive and organized.
> 3. Ignore distractions.

How Figure-Ground Relationship Works

The mind is so organized that from the totality of stimuli that is sent to it from all the senses, it can select and organize a central concept. All the other stimuli become less important and form varying degrees of background. The mind perceives most clearly what it turns its attention to. As the central concept, or figure changes and a new concept becomes central, the initial figure becomes less important and forms a part of the background.

Focus of attention is most critical in matters of figure-ground relationships. Almost any central concept cannot be perceived unless it is perceived in relation to its background. The distance, size and shape of objects can only be accurately perceived in relationship to their background. Thus, a bouncing ball can only be accurately retrieved by consideration of its background.

Figure-Ground relationships are essential in making sense out of the environment and the mass of stimuli constantly assaulting the senses in order to take appropriate action in a given situation.

SYMPTOMS OF FIGURE-GROUND RELATIONSHIP PROBLEMS

Inattention and Disorganization

Inattention is a term commonly used to describe a child with this problem. That is because his attention tends to jump to almost any stimulus that intrudes upon his perceptions. Anything that moves, glitters, shines or jiggles, no matter how irrelevant, commands his attention. It is not because he wants to, he simply cannot control himself. Conversely, this child often cannot direct his attention to the proper stimulus, causing others to perceive him as inattentive at the proper time to the proper things. "Stimulus Bound" is an appropriate term for children with this problem.

Stimulus Bound

Some of these children are "stimulus bound", that is, they cannot draw a line across another line to a point on the other side because their attention is captured and they direct their pencil along the crossing line. This child may return again and again to the origin of the lines so that his drawings make little or no sense. His letters are quite malformed.

Scanning

Schoolwork done by a child with this problem often appears extremely careless and messy. This occurs because he has extreme difficulty finding his place on a page, skips entire parts of the work, cannot find the right place to start or stop, or gets totally lost on pages with much detail. These children often seem unable to find anything, even if it right in front of them.

SIMPLE TESTS FOR FIGURE-GROUND RELATIONSHIP PROBLEMS

Hidden Picture Puzzles

From time to time children's magazines and puzzle sections of the newspaper contain hidden picture puzzles. It is a good idea to save some of them and use them for simple screening tests. Children love to do them and so they are easily motivated. They will try very hard to find the animals hidden in the clouds, trees or anyplace in the puzzle.

Sorting

Mix objects of two or more types together and have the child sort them. Objects may be sorted according to the size, shape, color or texture. They could also be sorted according to function depending on the intellectual level of the child.

Pen and Pencil Exercises

Mazes and dot-to-dot exercises along with almost any type of line drawing task could be a way of alerting an examiner to a stimulus bound child. A careful examination of the child's handwriting exercises or even arithmetic papers could show the difficulties this child might be experiencing.

GENERAL CLASSROOM ASSISTANCE

Material should be presented with minimum details. Assignments should be as simple as possible. Even normal amounts of material can be distracting to this child.

Blame-Guilt interactions must be avoided at all costs. The child with this problem is usually fully aware that he cannot perform certain assigned tasks and normal efforts at criticism can be exceptionally damaging. Many times this child has already given up by the time the problem is recognized. Attitudes arising from his success or failure can significantly affect his ability to perform.

Examples of Individual Remediation

Significant objects in pictures could be located, such as; types of flowers, insects, etc..

Frostig dittos. *

Hidden pictures. *

Find a square button in a box of round ones, a green marble among blue ones, a large block among small ones.

Dot-to-dot exercises. *

Hidden words in puzzles. *

Various categories could be sorted, such as: Red things, round things, small things, then specify objects such as a particular picture, toy or book. (Objects should become less and less conspicuous.)

Sorting: Two types of objects together, cubes, spheres, etc., then three types, then four types, etc..

Shifting attention: Particular objects are selected from boxes of many by touch, color, size, texture, etc..

Building models from plans. *

* Commercially available.

PERCEPTUAL CONSTANCY PROBLEMS

> What they are: Perceptual Constancy problems are failures to classify general properties of similar objects although they may be of varied shapes, sizes or colors. Children with this problem are often unable to:
> 1. Recognize numbers, letters or new words when they are presented in a new perspective.
> 2. Read cursive writing although they are well able to read printing.

How Perceptual Constancy Works:

The properties of perceptual constancy take the properties of real objects from patterns perceived by the senses. The mind makes generalizations from what is seen using the following cues:

1. Size, shape and brightness.
2. Perceptual modification.
3. Illusions from constancy failure.

This is dependent upon:

Sensory Input

Accurate data must be received from the senses so that reasonable judgments can be made at the unconscious level.

Training and Experience

The individual's environment and his past experiences determine what processing occurs. Prior perceptions create "set", or expectation, which often determines what is perceived.

The ultimate word recognition component of reading is Perceptual Constancy. Symbols and words must be recognized as having consistent identity regardless of the conditions in which they are seen. That is: An A must be recognized as an A even though it may be different colors, sizes or shapes, printed, written, small or large.

SYMPTOMS OF PERCEPTUAL CONSTANCY PROBLEMS

Letter Identification

In the initial stages of learning to read, children have difficulty distinguishing the forms of letters due to differences in form. Upper and lower case letters are not the same shape - A & a. Another element is added when the teacher's script is introduced - A, a and $\mathcal{a}$. A fourth element is added with cursive writing - A, a, $\mathcal{a}$ & $\mathcal{a}$. Children with difficulty in this area will be far behind normal development in letter identification.

Word Recognition

Children with this difficulty have a hard time with words that are very similar but have different meanings. Words written in different styles are very confusing to this child. Initially, cursive writing is next to impossible.

Confusion in New Surroundings

The narrowness of this student's experience in recognizing generalized similarities and his lack of practice in dealing with them leads to hesitancy and confusion. Children who have more than ordinary difficulty with new or strange surroundings or with new learning materials may be suspected of having this problem.

Spelling

Good spelling depends in part upon the perceptual constancy of words and in part upon the application of rules. Children who have difficulty in the area will most often have some difficulty with spelling.

SIMPLE TESTS FOR PERCEPTUAL CONSTANCY PROBLEMS

Flash Cards

Select approximately twenty words appropriate to the child's age and ability. Arrange them in order of increasing difficulty. Prepare two cards for each word, one in upper case and one in lower case, also one in cursive if appropriate.

Have the child match the cards noting hesitancies, lack of confidence, verbalization errors and time of performance (without mentioning timing.)

Compare with other children who do not appear to have this problem.

Sorting

Have the child sort buttons of different shapes and colors according to a graduated scale. This could also be done with nuts and bolts, screws or other age appropriate materials.

Present a collection of pictures of several different objects that vary in size, form, color or medium; photographs or abstract and representational drawings. Ask the child to sort them by classification and not the differences in color, size or shape.

GENERAL CLASSROOM ASSISTANCE

Working in new situations will be most difficult for a child with Perceptual Constancy Problems. Retaining familiar objects or routines in new situations will be most helpful in new situations or with new learning material.

Numbers, letters or words may be unrecognized when presented in new situations. Questioning the child in a very patient, non-threatening manner about his understanding of new material will be most helpful to make certain the child has perceived it properly.

Examples of Individual Remediations

Show circles of different sizes and ask: "Which is the little ball? Which is the big ball?" Go on to other objects which demonstrate height, weight, etc..

Differentiate large and small objects in the room. Have the child name large things: Tables, chairs, etc., and then name small things: Pencils, chalk, etc..

Present number concepts both in figures (1, 2, 3) and letters (one, two, three.) Also dots (., .., ...) and in Roman numerals (I, II, III)

As ability improves, present letters, words, sentences and in stories with different type styles and colors.

Exercises with two or three dimensional planes:

Show pictures of things built that resemble things built with blocks, brick or logs.

Match various shaped block to pictures of geometric form that are roughly similar.

Mix and match forms and pictures of similar objects.

BLENDING AND SEGMENTING PROBLEMS

> What they are: Blending and Segmenting problems are failures to see whole relationships as having a new identity different from the single parts that make up the whole. Blending is the process of grouping symbols into small units. Children with this problem are often unable to:
> 1. Tell the difference between words that are spelled alike but pronounced differently.
> 2. Understand that differing combinations of letters have the same sounds.

How Blending and Segmenting Works

Blending generally follows this pattern:
1. Organization of visual features in symbols.
2. Combination of two or more symbols into more complex patterns.
3. Development of symbolic patterns into parts of word, phrases and sentences.

Segmenting generally follows this pattern:
1. Organization of visual features into symbols.
2. Reduction of complex patterns into small symbols.

SYMPTOMS OF BLENDING AND SEGMENTING PROBLEMS

Mispronunciation

This is the simplest and probably the easiest symptom to identify. Unfortunately, it is also the most commonly overlooked. Even the simplest words can be pronounced incorrectly by this child when he is reading. Errors can be the same over and over, or they can be totally new.

Delayed Speech

Children who have this problem have trouble with common blends such as th, ph, pn, ie, ei or gh, do not find cues to meaning when the combinations are separated into individual letters and reblended.

Hesitancy

Significant pauses prior to or during the pronunciation of a word should lead to a closer analysis. Unusual pauses at the beginning of words or any place where combinations of letters having a single pronunciation are encountered are significant indicators of the problem, particularly when constantly observed.

Slow, Inaccurate Reading

Children with this problem do not read with confidence. They will read very slowly with many glances to see if they are on the right track. These children are very alert to criticism which has a damaging effect and can lead to regression in reading skill.

SIMPLE TESTS FOR BLENDING AND SEGMENTING PROBLEMS

Compound Words

Select line drawings of pairs of objects that will make compound words when combined. Arrange at least ten in increasing order of difficulty. (Sample): Picture of a boat, picture of a house. The child should make the verbal combination of a houseboat with a picture of a houseboat.

Slow Reading

Find the maximum success level of the child, (the level at which no mistakes are made) give a slightly more difficult reading exercise (the level at which two or more errors per line are observed) and compare with expected grade level performance. Children with problems in this area will be able to read accurately but with many errors along the way.

Spelling

Spelling exercises should be scanned for errors in blending and segmenting, reversals of letters or words.

GENERAL CLASSROOM ASSISTANCE

Extreme lack of participation and/or shyness is characteristic. Reading aloud should never be required, it should be encouraged. Mispronunciations are common and should never be made notice of in front of other children. Reading new and unfamiliar material requires much more time than average.

Examples of Individual Remediations

Use picture-word associations and start training with concrete associative words.

Use words that have consonant and sustained sounds; s, m, f, sh, r.
Proceed to those that are non-sustained: t, d, k, p.

Sight words taught as whole words: As, the, was.

Scrabble. *

Spill and Spell. *

Sound Alikes.

Phonetic rules of spelling.

Daily drill using the International Teaching Alphabet. *

The structural Reading Series. *

*Commercially available.

CHAPTER III

AUDITORY PROCESSING

CHILDREN WITH AUDITORY PROCESSING PROBLEMS

o   Mike has a very mercurial temperament. He is at times a very charming, pleasant child and at others a foul-mouthed, disobedient one who flies into rages for no apparent reason.

o   Jack has to have a personal direction for almost every classroom task. He seems incapable of following directions and seems to deliberately misbehave whenever he receives directions.

o   John is a "smart Alec" who never seems to pay attention to anything that is said. He would do or say anything to make his classmates laugh.

o   Talking to Walter is like talking to the air. In one ear and out the other describes him perfectly. He almost never remembers what is said.

All these are examples of children with auditory processing problems. These problems may be divided into four groups and will be described in the following order:
1. Sequencing
2. Memory
3. Abstraction
4. Discrimination

The same behaviors can be caused by different problems. When a child's behavior seems to suggest some processing problems be sure to check in other areas as well.

AUDITORY SEQUENCING PROBLEMS

> What they are: Auditory Sequencing problems are failures in the ability to retrieve auditory information in its proper sequence or order. Children with this difficulty are often unable to:
> 1. Recall auditory information in the order in which it was received.
> 2. Carry out a series of verbal directions.

How Auditory Sequencing Works

When auditory information is presented it is immediately and simultaneously sorted, classified and stored sequentially. This is dependent upon:

Perception

The ability to receive auditory information accurately and completely.

Attention

The ability to concentrate on specific stimuli while disregarding others

Organization

The ability to sort, classify, arrange and store information in the order in which it was received

Expectation

General preparation for what is to be heard, a "set". New material, unfamiliar material or unexpected material may or may not be completely retained.

Past Experience

The social, emotional and cognitive background of the individual.

SYMPTOMS OF AUDITORY SEQUENCING PROBLEMS

Lack of Attention

The child with this problem often appears not to pay attention to verbal directions. He continuously asks the teacher or other students to repeat assignments which have been given verbally. He frequently turns in assignments which are only partially completed and do not follow the sequence given.

Incomplete Work

Children with this problem frequently only partially complete assignments and fail to finish even the most simple tasks.

Indifference

Teachers often find students with this problem very aggravating because failure to follow even very simple verbal directions seems to be deliberate.

Lack of Motivation

These children seem not to care about the class, the teacher, the assignment or anything connected with school except socializing with their friends and/or extra-curricular activities.

Negative Response Pattern

As a defense for his inability to perform, a child with this problem may develop many negative or defiant behavior patterns. This seeming indifference cannot be changed by the usual punitive, corrective measures. This child often has already given up before his problem is noticed.

SIMPLE TESTS FOR AUDITORY SEQUENCING PROBLEMS

Number Repetitions

Prepare a series of numbers and letters beginning with three items, then four items, then five items and then six. Read these numbers to the child and ask him to repeat them immediately. If he seems to be depending on visual cues, face the child away from you. First say the numbers or letters forward, then backward.

Rhythm Patterns

Make up a series of rhythm patterns which might resemble the Morse Code. Tap out a series of three, then four, then five taps using a pencil tapping on a desk. Ask the child to tap out the same pattern.

Verbal Directions

Prepare a series of verbal directions that will require two, then three, then four steps to complete. They should be very simple directions so that the task can be completed in a minute or less. For example: Tell the child to write his name in the upper right corner of a paper, write the numbers one through ten on the left margin of the paper and place his name at the top of the paper.

GENERAL CLASSROOM ASSISTANCE

Directions given orally to this student should be repeated whenever necessary. The more simple and concise the auditory information dispensed, the more likely that communication will occur. Assignments and homework should be written down in detail and the teacher would be well advised to check the child's notes for logic and sequence.

Examples of Individual Remediations

Auditory Alphabet or counting games. *

Simple Simon game.

Taking orders for an imaginary drive-in, toy store or grocery store.

Spelling Bee. *

A dramatic play which requires the child to memorize several lines interrupted by other lines.

Poems or rhymes.

Memorizing songs for performance.

Naming the other children in the room in their seating order.

Computer games involving lists of number or letter sequence. *

Sequential flash cards. *

* Commercially available.

AUDITORY MEMORY PROBLEMS

> What they are: Auditory Memory problems are failures to recall information received from auditory cues. Children with this problem are often unable to:
> 1. Remember sounds that have meaning such as: bells, alarms, horns, whistles or music.
> 2. Remember letters, words, phrases or sentences.

How Auditory Memory Works

When auditory information is perceived it is sorted, classified, arranged and stored immediately and simultaneously. This is dependent upon:

Perception

The ability to receive accurate information.

Attention

The ability to focus on selected stimuli while disregarding others.

Screening

The ability to exclude specific distractions in the immediate environment.

Expectation

General preparation for what is to be heard, a "mind-set". New material, unfamiliar material or unexpected material may or may not be completely retained.

Experience

The unique prior social, emotional and cognitive reinforcements of the individual.

SYMPTOMS OF AUDITORY MEMORY PROBLEMS

Lack of Attention

A child with this problem often appears not to pay attention to verbal directions. He continuously asks the teacher or other students to repeat assignments which have been given verbally. When asked what has been said, he is often unable to give even the most remote interpretation, and this makes him seem not to have been paying attention.

Indifference

Teachers often find students with this problem very aggravating because the child doesn't seem to do what he is told. The child forgets, but to the teacher it seems as if he doesn't care about anything.

Repeated Instructions

Children with this problem will return again and again asking the teacher to explain something that has already been explained several times. Teacher can misinterpret this behavior as trying to "get" the teacher, when, in reality it is only a sincere effort to obtain information that has been forgotten because of the problem.

Disruption

Lectures or verbal explanations by the teacher are usually not retained. The child loses interest quickly and may, at times, be quite disruptive. Window gazing, whispering and general restlessness are characteristic of a child with this problem.

SIMPLE TESTS FOR AUDITORY MEMORY PROBLEMS

Stories

Have the child sit with his back to you so that he cannot receive visual or body language cues. Read him a short story with a sequence of at least three events. Ask him to repeat those events in as much detail as possible.

Nonsense Syllables

Prepare a series of nonsense syllables. Make sure none of them have any meaning at all. Begin with a series of three letter syllables, then four syllables then five. For instance:

fil	sada	clopa
los	ilma	lamas
maj	toma	putar

At least ten nonsense syllables should be included in each series. With the child facing you, say the first nonsense syllable and have him repeat it. Then, say the first and second and have him repeat them. Then, say the first, second and third syllables and have him repeat. Continue in this fashion until all the syllables are completed or the child has made obvious errors. Because of the number of repetitions the child will have memorized the early syllables quite thoroughly and retained at least five or six. Usually a disability in auditory memory is quite apparent very quickly in this test.

GENERAL CLASSROOM ASSISTANCE

Verbal directions and assignments should be kept as concise and simple as possible. Written directions and assignments should be substituted whenever possible. Assignments or directions given verbally should be checked to make sure they were retained. Ask: "What is the assignment?" Present material in context, in pairs, by association and in categories.

Examples of Individual Remediations

The child looks at a story as it is read.

Play add-on games: I'm going on a trip, I'm taking my _____. The next child repeats what he has heard and adds another item and so on.

Simon. *

Soundmaster. *

Speak and Spell. *

Poems.

Memorizing songs for performance.

Counting games.

Imitating animal sounds from tapes.

A picture is described, one item at a time. The child guesses which one it is from several on view. Items are added one at a time until the child gets it right.

Telling stories of tapes, records or TV shows.

Rhythm games.

Simon Says.

*Commercially available.

AUDITORY ABSTRACTION PROBLEMS

> What they are: Auditory Abstraction problems are failures to understand information received from auditory cues.
> Children with this problem are often unable to:
> 1. Maintain attention to auditory cues.
> 2. Select significant ideas from auditory information.
> 3. Achieve closure when auditory information is not complete.
> 4. Make accurate associations between what is heard and the meaning of that auditory information.

How Auditory Abstraction Works

When abstractions are made from auditory information they are not always sorted, classified and stored immediately. Prior organizations, experience and perceptions interact with current information to produce new abstractions which are then stored. This ability is dependent upon:

Perception

The ability to receive auditory information accurately with little or no distortion.

Attention

The ability to concentrate on specific stimuli while disregarding others.

Screening

The ability to select ideas appropriately in a specific situation for a specific purpose.

Reasoning

The level of ability to use inductive reasoning, deductive reasoning or similar thought processes. The level of ability to make logical assumptions and decisions.

SYMPTOMS OF AUDITORY ABSTRACTION PROBLEMS

Lack of Understanding

Children with this problem often miss meanings or fail to "get" explanations. They continuously ask teachers for explanations when given verbal directions. Teachers sometimes misunderstand this questioning and take it as a challenge. When a student asks for explanations of verbal directions more than occasionally, it might be well to think of it as a clue.

Failure to Obey

Failure to obey verbally given rules is an indication that should not be overlooked. A careful distinction should be made between the child with a behavior problem and one who might be having auditory abstraction problems.

Rule Violations

When do's and don'ts are given verbally, this student may remember them, be able to repeat them, but not understand their meaning and their application to his own behavior.

Lack of Response

Children with auditory abstraction problems can be very unresponsive. Some children are afraid of asking questions or calling attention to themselves for fear of displaying their failure to understand. A very quiet child who appears not to understand may well be worth some investigation for this learning problem.

SIMPLE TESTS FOR AUDITORY ABSTRACTION PROBLEMS

Logical Events

Prepare simple stories appropriate to the child's age level that have a very logical sequence of events. There should be several natural pauses in the action of the story that lead to logical following events. As you read the story, pause and ask the child: "What do you think comes next?" Failure to make a reasonable answer more than once or twice suggests some difficulty in this area.

Do's and Don'ts

When do's and don'ts are given verbally, careful questioning about their application will help to identify problems in auditory abstraction. When the child can clearly state what the do's and don'ts are in terms of his own behavior, he is demonstrating understanding. If he continues to ignore the stated guidelines it is obviously a behavior problem. If he cannot clearly state the rules in terms of his own behavior, or exhibits behavior that proves he does not understand the rules, an auditory abstraction problem should be suspected.

Songs

Practice some word game songs such as "Old MacDonald" with the entire class until most of the students are familiar with the sequence of appearance of the animal characters. Play the singing game with the child you are concerned about, stopping just before the introduction of a new character or the sound the animal makes. Ask the child to supply the correct information.

GENERAL CLASSROOM ASSISTANCE

The teacher might assign classroom responsibilities to the child. The child should be guided into thinking about cause and effect relationships. Deductive reasoning on a verbal level, including "why" questions, is helpful.

Examples of Individual Remediations

Have the child bring pictures and relate them to more than one area.

Ask the child to explain such questions as: Why do we have houses?

Have the child describe the main idea of a story just told.

The child teaches his favorite game to others.

Tell a story, pause frequently and have the child fill in the gaps.

Give directions that call for a response on the part of the child and make sure that understanding occurs.

Discuss the rights of others.

Stimulus-response exercises: What do we do when it rains? What should we do if we have a cold?

Have the child explain safety rules to others.

AUDITORY DISCRIMINATION PROBLEMS

> What they are: Auditory Discrimination problems are failures to tell the difference between sounds, including differences in intensity, intonation, timbre, frequency or pitch. Children with this problem are often unable to:
> 1. Perceive the subtle differences in sounds of letters in combination with other letters.
> 2. Perceive the difference in words that sound very similar but have different meanings such as: Merry, Mary and marry.

How Auditory Discrimination Works

Auditory information is actively interpreted and references drawn from this interpretation in an individual, selective manner. These individual differences are dependent upon:

Previous Experience

Each individual has received unique reinforcements of somewhat different character. These discriminations are usually at an almost automatic level, just below the threshold of consciousness. Prior reinforcement determines the kind and type of discrimination mechanism the individual possesses.

Interpretation

The mind is not a passive consumer of information. It actively constructs it own interpretations of information and draws inferences from them. The mind ignores some information and selectively attends to other information. Children with this problem demonstrate faulty interpretation of common stimuli.

Expectation

Intentions, plans, motivation and sustained interest are all aspects of previous "sets" or what the individual is expecting due to his unique previous experience. Discrimination of auditory information is a totally unique experience. The total strategy of the individual in the area of expectation is a requirement for understanding.

SYMPTOMS OF AUDITORY DISCRIMINATION PROBLEMS

Misunderstanding

A child with this problem will often misunderstand words in any task for which he is required to listen and respond. When these children are presented with a task in which the words are both unfamiliar and the meaning is unknown, misconceptions and mispronunciations will occur.

Missed Meanings

When this child is assigned an oral task in which he is required to listen and respond, he tends to have difficulty grasping the individual meanings, often mistaking one word for another. Directions given verbally to this child will often be misinterpreted because he missed some of the words or mistook them for other words. Sometimes it seems as if he is deliberately disobeying the instructions when, actually, he just misunderstood. Occasionally a child will be found who takes refuge in inaction for fear of making an error.

Poor Peer Relations

Verbal word games present a particularly difficult problem for children with this weakness. Other children who are playing the game become very impatient and can be quite cruel. Sometimes problems arise on the playground because this child said something offensive when, in fact, it was a total misunderstanding on the part of the child with the weakness.

SIMPLE TESTS FOR AUDITORY DISCRIMINATION PROBLEMS

Reading Aloud

Prepare a triple spaced copy of some familiar reading material such as "The Pledge of Allegiance" with the words well spaced out on the page. With the child facing away from you in order that he not receive any visual cues, have him read the material out loud. Using your copy, try to record exactly what the student really says without any prompting. If he goes faster than you can record, say something neutral such as; whoa, or whoa, wait a minute, I can't write that fast. Have him say the words again. Using a tape recorder can provide more detailed information.

Sound Alike Lists

Prepare a list of words that sound very much alike such as spear and spare. Say each pair to the child and have him repeat them, making careful notes of exactly how he says the words. A tape recorder is useful in case you are unable to record perfectly. Listening to the tape later may provide clues you may have previously missed.

GENERAL CLASSROOM ASSISTANCE

The child can be assisted in his understanding by note taking. The teacher should check frequently with the child to make certain that communication is taking place. This can be done very quickly by asking the child: "Is that clear?" or by having the child repeat the material or question in his own words. The child may be assisted by being seated close to or in front of the teacher.

Examples of Individual Remediation

Activities which require listening.

Activities which pair off similar sounds which the child discriminates. Gradually require more difficult discrimination until the whole words are paired. It may be helpful in the initial stage to use visual cues along with the auditory stimulus.

Numerals - Letters - Words
    Show - Say - Write - Recall
    Show - Say - Recall
    Say - Write - Recall
    Say - Recall

Sequence training: Months of the year, days of the week, poems, choral readings, stories, etc..

Begin a sentence and add to it. Each child repeats the sentence and adds something.

CHAPTER IV

VERBAL PROCESSING

CHILDREN WITH VERBAL PROCESSING PROBLEMS

o	Sam is a very agreeable child. He never complains or causes trouble. He goes along with everything and seldom requires any extra attention. He could be called "Silent Sam." He hardly ever speaks unless he absolutely must.

o	Sue is an enthusiastic follower. She will often enthusiastically second another child's idea or she often says: "Gee, I wish I said that." She seems to have a very limited capacity for expressing herself while, at the same time, she writes about the same events profusely.

o	John has extreme difficulty expressing himself. He often will start a sentence and then appear to be searching for the right word and fail to finish. His responses are fragmentary, minimal and largely inaccurate when asked to tell a story or relate some experience he has had.

o	Darla is a puzzle to her teacher. She seems so pretty, so eager, so bright-eyed, and yet when her teacher said good morning, she only smiled and seemed unable to respond. Darla was the apple of her mother's eye.

All of these children are examples of Verbal Processing problems. These problems may be divided into two groups and will be discussed in the following order:
1. Verbal Production
2. Verbal Response

VERBAL PRODUCTION PROBLEMS

> What they are: Verbal Production problems are failures to verbally express a quality and quantity of language appropriate for age and education. Children with this problem are often unable to:
> 1. Verbally express ideas accurately and completely.
> 2. Convey specific verbal meanings.
> 3. Speak in rich, descriptive language.

How Verbal Production Works

The complete expressive vocabulary is acquired from many sources including visual, auditory and abstract. It is sorted, classified, arranged and stored immediately and is subject to constant revision and modification from new data. This is dependent upon:

Perception

The ability to receive and comprehend language completely and accurately.

Organization

The ability to acquire, sort, classify, arrange and store language in appropriate and meaningful ways.

Pronunciation

The ability to use phonetic symbols correctly.

Physical Characteristics

Age appropriate physical mechanisms allowing clear, distinct and understandable language.

Experience

The unique social, emotional and cognitive background of the individual.

Retrieval

The ability to recall and express language appropriately, accurately and in a timely manner.

SYMPTOMS OF VERBAL PRODUCTION PROBLEMS

Verbal Non-communication

The most characteristic symptom of a child with this problem is almost total verbal non-communication. Every teacher has had at least one "Silent Sam." These children seem to go through life without needing to utter a word. A related type is the child who never speaks in the presence of strangers or authority figures but is voluble to intimate associates.

Paucity of Language

Some children with this problem have a very limited language. Because paucity of language is often an accompaniment to retardation it is important to make the distinction.

Delayed Speech

Occasionally children begin school with only a series of grunts, whistles, squeaks and gestures. Having their needs met in this fashion has made it unnecessary for them to use speech. Children who begin life in this way can demonstrate very limited verbal capacity in later life.

Catch Phrases

When a child uses phrases as a large part of his verbal communication, a limited vocabulary may be suspected. Give the child an opportunity for speaking spontaneously into a tape recorder. These tapes can determine weakness by the quality of the language.

SIMPLE TESTS FOR VERBAL PRODUCTION PROBLEMS

Sentences

Length and completeness of spoken language as well as syntax can be used as a comparative device. Have the child say at least ten sentences which use a single word cue such as; dog, chair, table or other, similar objects. A student with this problem will give very meager responses.

Tape Recording

Give the child the opportunity to speak spontaneously into a tape machine. This should be done in private and, when appropriate, without anyone present including the teacher. This will help in determining if the paucity of verbal language could be due to shyness rather than any verbal production problem.

Speech Evaluation

Careful attention in differentiating this problem should be paid to the speech processes themselves. Children with faulty speech do not necessarily have a verbal production problem. A referral to a speech specialist for diagnosis and treatment should be considered.

Animal Sounds

For very young children, reproducing the sounds of animals is a method of pre-screening verbal production. Tapes of those familiar sounds can be presented and the child asked to imitate them.

Story Telling

Have the child tell a story, or tell what happened on a favorite TV show. This can be done for the entire class or individually. Paucity of language will soon become apparent.

GENERAL CLASSROOM ASSISTANCE

A child with this problem will often not understand some of the words the teacher uses. The teacher should check often during verbal explanations to make sure this child understands. All types of reading should be encouraged and the child should be encouraged to discuss what he has read. The child should never be forced to perform verbally before his fellow students, however he might be encouraged to do so when appropriate.

Examples of Individual Remediations

Show and Tell.

The child repeats stories that other children tell.

The child describes his new TV show.

Group discussions.

Crossword puzzles at the appropriate age level.

Scrabble.*

Password. *

Analogy games. *

Dictionary work.

Have the child make up a word game. Require the other members of the class to play. The child can teach the game to all the players.

A part in a play which requires the student to memorize and engage in conversation with others.

Notebook kept by the student for new words.

Individual definitions of abstract words.

Panel discussions.

* Commercially available.

VERBAL RESPONSE PROBLEMS

> What they are: Verbal Response problems are failures to respond verbally to visual, auditory or other sensory cues in a pertinent, meaningful way. Children with this problem are often unable to:
> 1. Give an adequate verbal response to questions.
> 2. Maintain a conversation.
> 3. Read aloud with reasonable accuracy.
> 4. Verbally relate an adequate account of objects, events, or scenes they have experienced.

How Verbal Response Works

The verbal expression of previously sorted, classified and arranged material is a function of a series of immediate language search reactions to sensory cues. It is dependent upon:

Perception

The ability to recognize language in all forms with little or no distortion.

Organization

Retrieval of pertinent information is dependent upon how the information was sorted, classified and stored when it was received. Haphazard or incorrect storage makes retrieval difficult or impossible.

Selection

The ability to ignore irrelevant information is a necessary process when responding to cues. The mind is not passive, it is actively modifying all of its information and constructing its new information from the previous data it has received. Some individuals are simply unable to ignore irrelevant data and become unable to adequately respond to cues because they are lost in a myriad of possible responses to cues.

Experience

The unique social, emotional and cognitive prior reinforcement of the individual.

Background

Some individuals are unable to respond because the act of response has not been rewarded adequately or because the act of response has been punished.

SYMPTOMS OF VERBAL RESPONSE PROBLEMS

Social Isolation

Children with weakness in verbal response often are social loners in the classroom and on the playground because they have difficulty in carrying on conversations with other students. They often reply to cues by shrugging their shoulders, nodding their heads, using monosyllables or other inappropriate responses.

Incomplete Responses

This problem is often evidenced by short or incomplete responses. These children will often begin an answer only to trail off with irrelevant material or end in a whisper so that they do not have to finish.

Silent Participation

Children with this problem sometimes seem only to relate to others on a nonverbal level. They stand close to other people without saying anything or joining in the conversation. This silent participation reveals their interest and their desire to participate. In effect, they are participating even though it is at a nonverbal level. When teachers or others try to include them in the group or draw them out, they are quite inarticulate.

Inability to Read Aloud

This problem becomes very obvious when the child is required to read material aloud, either at his station or in front of the class. Care must be taken to separate performance anxiety from Verbal Response problems

SIMPLE TESTS FOR VERBAL RESPONSE PROBLEMS

Verbal Chaining

A chaining test of verbal response is easy to give and easy to record. Key words such as school, home, sister, brother, mother, father are used as stimulus words. The teacher might say: "I am going to say a word and I want you to tell me about it." Record the responses to each word. Inadequate responses will be quite obvious.

Visual Reporting

Show a film and ask the student to describe some part of the film and record the answers. This exercise for the whole class will help establish some standards that can be used for comparison. The words, phrases and syntax will reveal the student's facility with verbal response.

Touch Describing

A number of common objects are placed in a bag. The child is asked to place his hand in the bag and describe each object as it is touched. If the response is only the name of the object, the examiner might say: "Tell me more about it." Children with difficulties in this area will give limited responses, often omitting the most essential properties of the object.

Reading Aloud

Select any reading material that is appropriate for the particular individual. Make sure it is material that is easily within the reading range of the particular student. Have the student read the material **IN PRIVATE** out loud. Having the student perform in private will prevent shyness and fear of peer ridicule from interfering with the evaluation. If the student has previously demonstrated mastery of the material in some other modality, errors will soon become very obvious.

GENERAL CLASSROOM ASSISTANCE

Special care should be taken to avoid asking this child questions that require him to answer in front of other students. Reading aloud is a way of beginning to overcome the verbal inability to respond. Seating this child close to a child who has verbal abilities is recommended.

Examples of Individual Remediations

Show and Tell.

The child repeats stories that other children tell or stories the teacher tells.

Plays or stories with small speaking parts is which the child is required to consider the content of the part in order to respond.

Play store, the child is required to take orders and relay them to another child.

Panel Discussions.

Open End Discussions.

Word games in which the child is required to find the right word and say it aloud in order to move his marker ahead. Also, vowel games, consonant games or syntax games which are similar, depending on the level of the child.

Password Games. *

Analogy Games. *

Have the child make up his own word game. Require him to teach and play the game with other children.

Have the child tell about a recent movie or TV show.

Have the child tell about his favorite TV series, the characters in it and have him try to talk about the kind of show it is: adventure, detective, cartoon, soap, etc..

* Commercially available.

CHAPTER V

KINSESTHETIC PROCESSING

CHILDREN WITH KINESTHETIC LEARNING PROBLEMS

o   Brenda is a very pleasant girl. She is agreeable and follows directions quickly and well. Her performance on visual-motor tasks is very erratic, some things she does very well and others not at all.

o   Harry is the messiest kid in the class. He comes to school reasonably well dressed but it isn't very long before his shirt is half-out, his hands and knees dirty and his hair down in his eyes. Harry is awkward, he bumps, spills, drops, stumbles, slips and falls with constant regularity.

o   Jane's paperwork is usually covered with erasures and write-overs. Words are scratched out. When she is writing she cannot stay on the line, her letters are small and crowded together and her words waver up and down across the page, sometimes winding up with an upward sweep.

o   Bobby constantly reverses parts of words that he is copying. He has problems beginning work on the left side of the page of assignments. He seems to require visual cues in order to perform any task.

All of these children are examples of kinesthetic processing problems. For clarity and discussion these problems can be divided into four groups and will be described in the following order:

1. Kinesthetic Perception
2. Kinesthetic Coordination
3. Kinesthetic Learning
4. Kinesthetic Memory

KINESTHETIC PERCEPTION PROBLEMS

> What they are: Kinesthetic Perception problems are failures to perceive sequential relationships during sensory-motor activities. Children with this problem are often unable to:
> 1. Maintain laterality and directionality.
> 2. Keep written activities in order.
> 3. Read, write and spell in proper sequence.
> 4. Maintain proper spacing while writing.

How Kinesthetic Perception Works

As the individual engages in sensory-motor activity, the information received by the eyes, the ears and the proprioceptors is sorted, arranged and relayed to the involved sensory-motor areas simultaneously. This is dependent upon:

Perception
The ability to receive kinesthetic information accurately.

Physical Processes
Age appropriate physical development allowing adequate physical performance.

Organization
The ability to sort, classify and arrange appropriately.

Concentration
The ability to focus on specific stimuli while disregarding others.

Experience
The unique social, emotional and cognitive background of the individual.

SYMPTOMS OF KINESTHETIC PERCEPTION PROBLEMS

Directionality

Children with this problem have difficulty in working from left to right on a page. They reverse parts of words they are copying. They often make mistakes in written spelling such as; tsrng, or stnrg for string. They will also make the same sort of errors in reading because their ability to perceive this information is faulty.

Laterality

Even after repeated directions, a child with this problem has a difficulty beginning work on the left margin of papers. Problems in proper spacing are constant.

Physical Directionality

Often children with this problem can be see "bucking the traffic". They seem unable to keep to the right when going down hallways or going through doors. Even after specific and repeated directions, the pattern remains.

SIMPLE TESTS FOR KINESTHETIC PERCEPTION PROBLEMS

Games

A game such as "Simon Says" is a simple test for young children. Children with this problem will be dependent upon observing others when trying to comply with directions such as: Simon says, put your hand on your head. Or, Simon says, put your hand on your shoe. A child who demonstrates difficulty with games of this sort very likely has a kinesthetic perception problem.

Sequential Written Directions

Sequential written directions such as: Put the page number in the upper right-hand corner of your paper, write your name in the upper left hand corner, and number every other line on the left hand side of the paper are real problems for children with this difficulty. Almost any program of age appropriate sequential directions will reveal a weakness in this area.

GENERAL CLASSROOM ASSISTANCE

Exercises using three dimensional objects such as blocks or Origami are most helpful. Try to have paper and pencil work after some three dimensional activity. Special attention should be given when written sequencing activities are required to see that this child begins the work properly.

Examples of Individual Remediations

Stringing Beads. *

Pegboards. *

Reading Maps.

Yard work activities involving a series of events.

Dot-to-Dot. *

Trace incomplete drawings, completing them. *

Age appropriate puzzles. *

Have the child present alternate routes to and from school, home or other places of interest.

Assembling Blocks. *

Have the child develop planned, sequential activities for class projects, plays or parties.

Any kind of building according to plans.

Give complex directions to physical activities. Require the child to complete at extreme speed.

* Commercially available.

KINESTHETIC COORDINATION PROBLEMS

> What they are: Kinesthetic Coordination problems are failures in sensory motor coordination, including both large and small muscle coordination. Children with this problem are often unable to:
> 1. Stay on lines when writing.
> 2. Complete a paper without many errors in shaping letters and placement of sentences.
> 3. Participate well in physical sports.
> 4. Catch a ball easily.

How Kinesthetic Coordination Works

As the individual engages in sensory motor activity, the information received by the eyes, the ears and the proprioceptors is coordinated and relayed to the involved sensory motor areas immediately and simultaneously. This is dependent upon:

Perception

The ability to receive sensory motor information accurately.

Motor Coordination

The movement of muscles and the positioning of the skeletal support in response to sensory cues. An orderly sequence of smooth motions that is both rhythmic and controlled is essential to this process.

Physical Processes

Age appropriate physical development allowing adequate physical performance. Optical, neuro-muscular, skeletal and otological functions must be at or near operational levels of maturation.

Concentration

The ability to focus on a specific stimuli while disregarding others.

SYMPTOMS OF KINESTHETIC COORDINATION PROBLEMS

Awkwardness

The primary behavior symptom of the child with kinesthetic coordination weakness is a noticeable awkwardness in physical movements. This child bumps into things, spills, knocks things over, and drops things. He often seems to be "all thumbs" and seems to have two left feet.

Difficulty in Sports

A child with this problem has difficulty playing organized games on the playground. In baseball, he swings the bat awkwardly, seldom getting a hit. He often misses ball hit or thrown directly at him. Because of this dysfunction and consequent problems in games of this type, other children usually don't want to play with them and many times they are among the last to be chosen for team sports.

SIMPLE TESTS FOR KINESTHETIC COORDINATION PROBLEMS

Ball Bouncing

A very simple test for all ages is ball bouncing. Even a kindergarten child should be able to bounce a ball at least once. As children grow older, smaller and smaller balls could be used.

Drawing

Prepare dot-to-dot or numbered drawings of age level shapes. Note the difficulties the child may have drawing straight lines. False starts and starts that do not begin at a dot are significant. Difficulties in changing directions are also important.

Games

Playschool games with geometric shapes and match holes are also useful. Watch the child carefully and take detailed notes. The material produced in these games is often very significant in determining the child's ability level in this area.

Writing

Exercises that involve formation of letters, or, in older children, spelling or writing sentences will reveal difficulties in this area.

GENERAL CLASSROOM ASSISTANCE

Written work done by a child with this weakness may be unnecessarily messy or disorganized. When possible, the seeming lack of care which is evidenced should be ignored. Due to the child's rigidity in approaching new materials he may experience difficulty in accomplishing grapho-motor assignments. Therefore, this child should be given extra time to complete written or copy assignments.

Examples of Individual Remediations

Jigsaw puzzles at appropriate age levels. *

Flannel board activities.

Picture Tracing.

Sewing cards. *

"Chinese" wooden puzzles. *

Copying simple designs.

Learning the Morse Code. *

Learning the U.S. Navy signal flag system.

Weaving.

Macrame. *

Typing.

Chinese Checkers. *

Plastic light board pictures. *

Baseball or other sports.

Pemanship exercises.
Origami. *

* Commercially available.

KINESTHETIC LEARNING PROBLEMS

> What they are: Kinesthetic Learning problems are failures to learn using sensory motor skills. Children with this problem are often unable to:
> 1. Reproduce numbers, letters or words well.
> 2. Reproduce shapes, patterns or designs well.
> 3. Learn material well by writing.
> 4. Spell accurately.

How Kinesthetic Learning Works

As the individual engages is sensory motor activity, the information received by the eyes, the ears and the proprioceptors is sorted, classified, arranged and stored immediately at a subconscious level. This is dependent upon:

Perception

The ability to receive sensory motor information accurately and completely.

Physical Development

Optical, neuro-muscular, skeletal and otological development must be at or near normal maturational levels.

Organization

The ability to sort, classify and arrange sensory motor information accurately.

Experience

The unique social, emotional and cognitive background of the individual.

SYMPTOMS OF KINESTHETIC LEARNING PROBLEMS

Messy Work

A child with this problem has a great deal of difficulty performing any written work. It will be full of errors and erasures. Writing will be off the lines and the formation of letters will be of many different sizes and shapes. Shaping of letters takes much time and effort, consequently the connections between letters are often very poor.

Poor Art Projects

This child's art projects will usually be very messy. Folding, pasting, cutting and coloring are areas of great difficulty for this child. He often complains: "I can't ..." and tends to give up easily when any complex manipulation of material is involved.

Disruptive Behavior

A child with this problem will most often do anything that is successful in avoiding tasks that call for use of this skill. Spelling, for example, is to be avoided whenever possible, by whatever means possible. It is important to take notice of what events are occurring when the disruptive behavior occurs. The timeliness should give the teacher a clue.

SIMPLE TESTS FOR KINESTHETIC LEARNING PROBLEMS

Observation of Written Work

Looking at the written work of a student with this weakness is a simple test. The problem will be apparent at first glance. Poorly formed letters, poor connections between letters along with many errors and erasures will be readily apparent. Written work by this child appears messy and disorganized even with very cursory examination.

Copying Designs

Age appropriate materials involving circles, squares, diamonds, and similar figures should be made available for this child to copy. The older the child the more increasing complexity is called for. Inspection of the work will reveal the difficulty in connecting lines, the misperception of the figures, and the generally haphazard placement of the copied figures. The entire work will probably be messy.

Reproducing Designs

This child will have a great deal of difficulty reproducing designs on light boards, peg boards, geo boards and other similar devices.

GENERAL CLASSROOM ASSISTANCE

Children with this problem should be allowed extra time to complete written or copied assignments. Great care should be exercised so that they are not penalized for work errors involving this weakness. Improvement in this skill is very slow and expectations should be minimal. As always, praise for good work is very motivating.

Examples of Individual Remediations

Cutting Exercises

The tactile alphabet. The child traces the letters with his eyes closed and reproduces them in mid-air.

Template training of beginning form perception. The child copies or traces and reproduces with his eyes closed. Gradually increase difficulty.

Perceptual Bingo. *

Sewing Cards. *

Lacing Cards. *

Visual motor templates for tracing basic forms.

Use acetate overlays in a sequential set of materials. The steps should be very gentle, from the simple to the complex.

Parquetry design cards. *

Pegboard exercises. *

Filmstrips which will reinforce different perceptually skills of basic forms such as; figure-ground, spacial relations, etc..

Lite Brite. *

Motor generalization training as Kephart, Getman methods. These are gross motor area training methods.

* Commercially available.

KINESTHETIC MEMORY PROBLEMS

> What they are: Kinesthetic Memory problems are failures to recall material or physical acts learned through the use of sensory-motor skills. Children with this problem are often unable to:
> 1. Recall patterns, shapes or designs.
> 2. Recall numbers, letters, words or sentences.
> 3. Remember what they have written.
> 4. Remember physical routines.

How Kinesthetic Memory Works

As the individual engages in sensory-motor activity, the information received by the eyes, the ears and the proprioceptors is sorted, classified, arranged and stored immediately at the sub-conscious level. This is dependent upon:

Perception

The ability to receive sensory-motor information accurately and completely.

Physical Processes

Age appropriate development allowing adequate physical performance.

Organization

The ability to sort, classify, arrange and store sensory-motor information appropriately.

Concentration

The ability to focus on specific stimuli while disregarding others.

SYMPTOMS OF KINESTHETIC MEMORY PROBLEMS

Forgetting Simple Physical Routines

Children with this problem often have difficulty remembering how to open or close desk tops, how to fold, cut, tear or wrap and many other simple physical tasks.

Materials Missing

This child will often show up for small group activities with some of the needed material missing. He will forget that he needs a pencil, paper or something of that sort even though he has participated in the physical routine many times.

Messy Work

A child with this weakness often appears to be messy. His work habits are haphazard and somewhat disjointed. He never seems to know what to do first. He has trouble finding his place in the book.

Following Rules

This child does not line up with the other children. He fails to put his belongings in their proper place and precipitates quarrels with other kids because he has taken the wrong place for his things. These behaviors are often disruptive and special care should be taken to determine if the behavior is simply an attention getting device or is a symptom of weakness.

SIMPLE TESTS FOR KINESTHETIC MEMORY PROBLEMS

Games

With very young children, the game of Old MacDonald can be used by watching the child as he imitates the physical routines of other children. Can he remember the physical routines of others and reproduce them accurately? Give these suspected children the chance to be "it" in small groups so that the memory of imitation is called for.

A device for older children is the game of follow the leader. This game will demonstrate immediate recall of physical routines. A child with this problem will often miss when his turn to follow the leader comes. In this way he will usually lose the game by being unable to do what is demonstrated.

Daily Classroom Routine

A very valuable test is the teacher's knowledge of what is average behavior in the normal physical routine of the classroom. A child with this problem usually stands out prominently when it comes to learning simple physical routines which are a change from past behavior.

GENERAL CLASSROOM ASSISTANCE

Students with this disability are often unable to remember physical routines and many times must be reminded. It is important to understand that this forgetfulness is not intentional. A special notebook for this child would be most helpful for those common routines which are a daily occurrence. Providing visual cues for physical tasks is very helpful. Designating another child for observation by a child with this problem can save much time.

Examples of Individual Remediations

The tactile alphabet, letters are traced blindfolded and reproduced in the air. Very gently and very gradually, train to pantomime.

Training in body concepts and body awareness.

Have the child learn to accompany his verbal expression with motor expression.

Visual-motor templates for tracing basic forms and reproducing from memory.

The game of Concentration. *

Pegboard exercises. *

Lite Brite. *

Parquetry. *

"Chinese" wooden puzzles. *

Jigsaw puzzles at appropriate age levels.

Learning the U.S. Navy flag semaphore system.

Learning the telegrapher's code.

Origami, repeat designs from memory.

Macrame.

* Commercially available.

CHAPTER VI

ABSTRACT PROCESSING

CHILDREN WITH ABSTRACT PROCESSING PROBLEMS

o   Tina is a happy girl who drifts through life with a sweet smile and seems to have no cares. She has trouble with switches, knobs, tools and other somewhat complicated objects.

o   Charlie is a pleasant young boy who is most anxious to be helpful to teachers and other students. He learns everything by rote. Once he learns how to solve a problem he never forgets, but plans and written directions just don't seem to get through.

o   Bonnie is an extremely charming child with many ways of relating well with other children and adults. She flits from task to task almost endlessly, she is always busy, but at different tasks.

All of these children are examples of Abstract Processing problems. For the purpose of clarity and understanding they will be divided into three groups and presented in the following order:

1. Integrative Learning
2. Non Verbal Concept Formation
3. Concentration

INTEGRATION LEARNING PROBLEMS

> What they are: Integration Learning problems are failures to coordinate or integrate different modes of intellectual reasoning in reference to a single problem. Children with this problem are often unable to:
> 1. Understand problems with multiple concepts.
> 2. Carry out complex directions.
> 3. Retain meanings from multi-modal material.

How Integration Works

When multi-modal material is presented it is sorted, classified, arranged and stored in appropriate categories. The interaction between modes is a reference point for recall of each or every part. This is dependent upon:

Perception

The ability to receive accurate sensory information.

Experience

The unique social, emotional and cognitive prior events of the individual.

Selection

The ability to ignore irrelevant information. The mind is not passive, it is actively modifying its information from current data and conscious or sub-conscious intellectual processing.

Retrieval

The ability to recall previously stored information accurately and in its proper order.

SYMPTOMS OF INTEGRATIVE LEARNING PROBLEMS

Reading without meaning

Children with problems in integrative learning can read aloud with reasonable accuracy, but when they are asked what they have read it becomes obvious that they did not understand the meaning of the selection.

Verbal Directions

A child with this problem when given verbal directions is unable to carry out the prescribed task, even when he can repeat the directions verbatim. This child must be shown exactly what to do by concrete demonstration and on a step by step basis.

Multiple Concept Problems

Children with this problem take a long time to catch on to the "trick" of reading though they may be able to decode with some success. Written expression is also difficult for them. In later years they have some difficulty writing themes, term papers and answering essay questions on written exams.

Multiple Use Mechanisms

Individuals with problems in integration have great difficulty using mechanical devices with multiple functions. Electric switches which can be pushed, pulled, flipped or twisted are never quite mastered. Driving automobiles can be quite hazardous. Inappropriate tools such as knife points or fingernails for a screwdriver are often used, usually with poor results. The obvious use of tools must be demonstrated or taught.

SIMPLE TESTS FOR INTEGRATIVE LEARNING PROBLEMS

Reading a Story

Have the child read a short story, appropriate to his age, out loud. Then ask him to tell the story. Children with difficulty in integrative learning can't remember much of what they have just read.

Sound Alike Words

Prepare lists of words to be read that sound alike but are spelled differently such as there and their, or words that are pronounced alike but have different meanings such as merry, marry and Mary. Have the student explain the differences. students with problems in this area will experience great difficulty performing the task.

Groups of Objects

Make lists of groups of objects with three objects the same and one different, such as three oranges and one apple. Another type of list would be groups of objects with something in common, such as an apple, an ice cream cone, a lollipop and one item different such as a baseball. Have the child explain the difference or the similarities. Any one of several answers could be right. Children with problems in this area will demonstrate their weakness.

Types of Response

Sometimes, how the student responds is just as important as the response. Is he hesitant? Does he give a quick, thoughtless answer? Does he give up easily? Does he give a slow, considered answer? Careful notation of what is said is most important.

GENERAL CLASSROOM ASSISTANCE

When giving directions the teacher should stress the concrete rather than the abstract until the ability to deal with abstraction improves. Language should be as clear and concise as possible in each situation. Analytical thinking should be encouraged.

Examples of Individual Remediations

The child acts out emotions: happy, sad, angry, etc..

Show objects which are unlike each other but have the same function such as airplanes and birds, fish and boats. Have the child guess the function.

Discuss concepts such as redness, roundness.

Have the student make scrapbooks in different categories.

Match abstract concepts with concrete pictures; a mother holding a child = love, clowns = happy.

Topographical similarities and differences: Lakes, rivers and oceans, mountains and hills.

Teach the child to generalize logically.

Have the child develop lists of opposites and differences.

Similarities and differences in geometric designs could be discussed.

Have the child develop various classification such as kinds of animals, functions of tools, using dictionaries, encyclopedias or other reference materials.

Abstract discussions: liberty, freedom, minority, etc..

Basic scientific experiments of a concrete nature: the electrolysis of water, etc..

NON VERBAL CONCEPT PROBLEMS

> What they are: NonVerbal Concept problems are failures to form concepts below the verbal level, to plan and to understand without verbal direction. Children with this problem are often unable to:
> 1. Understand how machines work.
> 2. Read plans or blueprints.
> 3. Comprehend the meaning of a look or gesture.

How Non Verbal Formation Works

When non verbal material is presented it is sorted, classified, arranged and stored immediately, usually below the level of consciousness. This is dependent upon:

Perception

Visual, auditory, tactile and proprioceptive senses must be capable of transmitting accurate information.

Organization

The ability to arrange and store information in appropriate and meaningful ways.

Selection

The ability to ignore irrelevant information.

Experience

The unique social, emotional and cognitive background of the individual as it relates to specific information.

Retrieval

The ability to recall appropriate information for a specific situation.

SYMPTOMS OF NON VERBAL CONCEPT FORMATION PROBLEMS

Simple Project Errors

Children who have problems in this area will make constant errors in the most simple projects. They will constantly ask for explanations of "how to do it" for each step along the way.

Repeated Demonstration

Simple art projects such as making a small basket or weaving a hot pad require repeated demonstration and/or explanation. Sometimes even when the project is completed this child winds up with a very crudely fashioned product, showing how much difficulty they have with understanding the principles of a project.

Necessity for Plans

Even with plans, a child with difficulty in this area is incapable of completion of a project without precise details. If any detail is not totally explained, or if some detail is left out, this child is hopelessly lost and unable to proceed.

Mechanical Device Mysteries

Mechanical devices are total mysteries to individuals with this problem. Autos, can openers, light switches, washing machines and other common household devices are totally incomprehensible and breakdown of these devices is regarded as a catastrophe. Individuals with this problem regard mechanical devices as their mortal enemies.

Body Language Understanding

Looks, gestures and postures which have a specific meaning are seldom understood. Lack of response to these actions is often misunderstood by associates as lack of interest.

SIMPLE TESTS FOR NON VERBAL CONCEPT FORMATION PROBLEMS

Folding Demonstration

Any simple folding exercise that requires observation and duplication. Origami, or folding a paper airplane might be good examples.

Using Mechanical Devices

A child suspected of having this problem could be asked to empty the pencil sharpener. A demonstration of removal and replacement of the container should be made without verbal instruction. A child who has trouble in this area will require repeated demonstrations and a lot of trial and error learning.

Combination Locks

For older children, simple three number combination locks present serious problems to those who have difficulty in this area. Some students and even some adults require considerable assistance is coping with this device. Their usual report of difficulty is "I forgot the combination", when the real problem is that they cannot work the lock. Performance is this area is easily judged.

GENERAL CLASSROOM ASSISTANCE

Relationships should be stressed. Tying together small pieces of information in different areas to form meaningful wholes is necessary. This child tends to learn small pieces at a time rather than whole concepts. Therefore, the teacher should check carefully to see that the child understands the entire idea being presented. Directions should emphasize the concrete.

Examples of Individual Remediations

Exercises in tracing and coloring within lines.

Form Board exercises. *

Origami.

Paper cutting and folding.

Puzzles appropriate to age. *

Sorting activities.

Drawing activities, copying and freehand.

Finding hidden figures in pictures.

Spirogram. *

Reconstructing jumbled sentences.

Separating real words from nonsense words.

Reading charts, maps or graphs.

Sorting objects, pictures or symbols for concepts.

Model building without plans.

Teaching the child to comprehend his environment is a way of teaching him to understand what he sees. Prepare questions about certain places and ask the child to go there and bring back his answers.

* Commercially available.

CONCENTRATION PROBLEMS

> What they are: Concentration problems are failures to pay attention to specific stimuli for given periods of time. Children with this problem are often unable to:
> 1. Remain on task for appropriate times.
> 2. Focus attention in distracting situations.
> 3. Ignore non pertinent stimuli.

How Concentration Works

Concentration is the active selection process in which the individual is clearly aware of specific stimuli at a given time. This is dependent upon:

Perception
The ability to receive information accurately.

Screening
The ability to be aware of specific stimuli while disregarding others.

Needs
The physical and emotional requirements of the individual at any given moment.

Interests
The personal preferences of the individual for areas of preferred activity.

Experience
The unique social, emotional and cognitive background of the individual as it relates to specific stimuli.

Alertness
The level of current awareness of environment and the intellectual interaction with it.

SYMPTOMS OF CONCENTRATION PROBLEMS

Chattering

A child with concentration problems is usually one who talks when he should be working. A great deal of time is wasted trying to get the child to stop talking. The effort is usually wasted because the problem is not the talking, it is the lack of ability to attend to the task.

Changing Behaviors

A child with this problem is distracted by any unusual noise or event and jumps to investigate. After the new stimulus is investigated this child ha a difficult time returning to the original task. This disorderly process of changing behaviors is so random that it is difficult to follow.

Copying

In an attempt to catch up on work that hasn't been finished because of random behavior, copying other students and/or cheating is not uncommon.

Disruption

Children with this problem are almost continuously disruptive. It is not intentional and does not have an emotional overtone. It is simply the result of distractibility and should not be confused with hyperactivity although they are many times found together.

Short Attention Span

A child with this problem has a mind like a butterfly. It jumps from concept to concept with no apparent relationship. The time spent on task is extremely short. Distractibility is the result, not the cause.

SIMPLE TESTS FOR CONCENTRATION PROBLEMS

Repeating Numbers, Letters or Words

In a quiet place away from distracting stimuli, tell the child to write down what you are going to say. Have a series of numbers, at an age appropriate level, prepared in advance. The series could also be letters or words, but it should be long enough to give the child's attention time enough to wander.

Reading Tests

Any reading test which has a follow-up comprehension test appropriate to the age level should give an indication of ability to concentrate. Although many other areas are also being tested, one important component is the ability to concentrate.

Thought Problems

Age appropriate arithmetic problems that have to be accomplished without the aid of paper and pencil can give a indication of the extent of the ability to concentrate.

Telling Stories

Someone in the class tells a story and afterward asks questions. These questions could be answered by each child in writing, thus giving not only a measure of the child suspected having this problem, but also a measure of what the average child might answer.

GENERAL CLASSROOM ASSISTANCE

The child should be given relatively short tasks, gradually lengthened as the ability improves. The time will vary with individuals and interest in the given area. Directions should be short and precise with follow-up to see that understanding has taken place.

Sample Individual Remediations

Present groups of objects and suggest concepts of more, least, less, etc..

Have the child trace, copy, match or name geometric shapes.

The child matches similar sets by number of class.

Use clock face and calendar for ideas of time.

Suggest concepts of measurement by using ruler, tapes, money, weights, etc..

Ideas of first, last, second, etc., can be taught in the lining up of children, taking turns and other similar activities.

Longer and longer tasks of concrete nature should be devised, depending on individual progress.

Graph exercises of increasing complexity.

Ideas of equality and inequality should be introduced.

Concrete objects could be used for demonstration.

Drill and practice of facts is a necessity. Making the practice interesting presents a challenge. Batting averages could be figured, bowling averages, approximate cost of maintaining a household - groceries, rent, car payment, etc..

Flannel board material, block and cut-outs could be used to increase time span.

Do not take the child's knowledge of basic facts for granted. Review subject matter frequently.

CHAPTER VII

REMEDIATIONS

REMEDIATION PLANS

A remediation plan for specific learning process problems requires three parts:

1. Remediation exercises for the specific learning process problems.

2. Selected phonics training.

3. Tutoring at the individual's level.

Remediating the Learning Process Problem

Students with learning process problems habitually avoid tasks which require use of their problem area, probably because it is psychologically painful for them to perform tasks which they can't do well. This avoidance takes many forms. It can be acting out, classroom mischief, poor academic performance, withdrawal or many other avoidance mechanisms. Because of this avoidance behavior, very subtle means must be employed in order to achieve improvement in weak learning process areas. Playing games which require use of the weak learning process is a way of arriving at this goal. Great care must be taken to make certain the game selected is itself not painful to the child. If any dissatisfaction is noticed, stop the activity at once! Go on to another activity that is not painful to the child. Considerable attention must be exercised to insure that the activities selected for remedial work are not perceived by the child as onerous or painful. Unpleasant activities only make the problem worse.

Included in other parts of this text are lists of suggested activities to improve weak learning process areas. A first step in devising a remedial program is to select a number of activities which might be considered fun or pleasant by the individual who is to perform them. The lists included in this text are intended as guides and remedial plans might properly include activities which are similar but not listed.

Phonics Training

When a student has a learning process problem, much of regular education is not assimilated. As soon as the learning process begins to show improvement in the remedial area, efforts should be started to replace the missing elements in the child's educational inventory. A major part of this inventory is the ability to use phonics effectively, and this ability is often severely hampered by a learning process problem. A remediation plan which does not include an effort to replace what has not been learned, in many cases phonics, has little promise of assisting the child in achieving his full potential. The best available phonics program should be used.

Tutoring

Tutoring must be at the individual's achievement level, not classroom make-up work. The student must have success experiences in this activity. Often, efforts at tutoring are directed at the individual's classroom work. This is usually a serious error when learning process problems are evident since the child has probably given up on this experience through a long trial and error effort.

SUMMARY

All three components: Remediation, Phonics training and Tutoring are necessary if children with learning process problems are to be brought to their individual ability potential. These three components must be used consecutively, and only after progress has been demonstrated in each one. Elimination of any one of the components results in significant lack of improvement.

Assessment of progress should be a continuous process. Much damage can be done by continuing an activity when the desired objective has been achieved. The assessment process should be looked upon as something like driving a car on a trip. One should expect to make many small corrections, to take alternative routes when roadblocks are reached, to estimate times when key points of progress can be attained, to follow rules of the signals and to make the proper turns that assure eventual arrival at the goals set.

A clear look at results is most important. Sometimes evaluation has taken on the aspects of a court trial with an accuser and a defendant in which someone must be blamed and a punishment meted out. In evaluation the real question that must be asked is: Did it work or didn't it? If it worked, celebrate! If it didn't, change it! Constant evaluation is an integral part of a remedial program for a child with a learning process problem.

Fortunately, learning process skills are, for the most part, learned behaviors. Whatever has been learned can usually be unlearned and retaught. If the plans given in this text are carefully followed, real progress can be expected from children who have previously been passed over without any real idea of what to do. Now the way is clear. Children with learning process problems can be brought back to their full potential.

BIBLIOGRAPHY

Aaron, P.G. A neuropsychological key approach to diagnosis and remediation of learning disabilities. *Journal of Clinical Psychology*, 1978, 35, 326 - 335.

Ames, K.N. Sensory organization and learning - - it works! *Academic Therapy*, 1979, 14, 327-333.

Aukerman, R.C. *Approaches to Beginning Reading.* New York: John Wiley & Sons, Inc., 1971.

Ball, T.S. Itard, Seguin and Kephart: *Sensory education - - a learning interpretation.* Columbus, Ohio: Charles E. Merrill Publishing Company, 1971.

Barbe, W.B., Swassing, R.H., & Milone, M.N. Teaching to modality strengths: Don't give up yet! *Academic Therapy*, 1981, 16, 262-266.

Benton, A.L. Dyslexia: Evolution of a Concept. *Bulletin of the Orton Society*, 1980, 30, 10 - 26.

Benton, A.L. & Pearl, D. (Eds.). *Dyslexia.* New York: Oxford University Press, 1978.

Brooks, C.H. A combined phonics and multisensory approach promotes reading improvement. *Reading Improvement*, 1975, 12, 87-93.

Brooks, J.D. The effects of a remedial reading program upon selected reading students in the fourth, fifth and sixth grades (Doctoral dissertation, East Texas State University, 1976). *Dissertation Abstracts International*, 1977, 37, 6920A. (University Microfilms No. 77-90-623)

Bryant, S.T. Relative effectiveness of visual-auditory versus visual-auditory-kinesthetic-tactile procedures for teaching sight words and letter sounds to young, disabled readers (Doctoral dissertation, cloumbia University Teachers College, 1979). *Dissertation Abstracts International*, 1979, 40, 2588A. (University Microfilms No. 79-24-584)

California Achievement Tests. Technical Bulletin I. Monterey, California: McGraw-Hill, 1979.

Clarke, L. *Can't read, can't write, can't talk too good either.* New York: Penguin Books, 1973.

Clinkert, R.J. Language competency, dyslexia and learning disability. *Bulletin of the Orton Society*, 1978, 28, 208-216.

Cook, J.E., Nolan, G.A., & Zanotti, R.G. Treating auditory perception problems: The NIM helps. *Academic Therapy*, 1980, 15, 473-481.

Critchley, M. *The dyslexic child.* London: William Heinemann Medical Books Ltd., 1978

Critchley, M. & Critchley, E.A. *Dyslexia defined.* London: William Heinemann Medical Books Ltd., 1978.

Duane, D.D., & Rawson, M.B. (Eds.) *Reading, perception and language.* Baltimore: York Press, 1975.

Early, G.H., & Kephart, N.C. Developing perceptual-motor skills: Perceptual-motor training and academic achievement. *Academic Therapy Quarterly*, 1969, 4, 201-206.

Eaton, I.E. The relationship between perceptual-motor ability and reading success (Doctoral Dissertation, Saint Louis University, 1975). *Dissertation Abstracts International*, 1975, 36, 3562A, (University Microfilms No. 75-26-249)

Ellison, L.H. A comparative study of the Fernald reading method and systematic desensitization as methods to improve readign achievement in learning disabled children (Doctoral dissertation, University of South Carolina, 1977). *Dissertation Abstracts International*, 1978, 38, 5391A. (University Microfims No. 78-01-141)

Fernald, G.M. *Remedial techniques in basic school subjects.* New York: McGraw-Hill, 1943.

Fisher, D.F. Compensatory training for disabled readers: Research to practice. *Journal of Learning Disabilities*, 1980, 13, 25-31.

Frauenheim, J.G. A follow-up study of adult males who were clinically diagnosed as dyslexic in childhood (Doctoral dissertation, Wayne State University, 1975). *Dissertation Abstracts International*, 1975, 36, 2741A. (University Microfilms No. 75-25-240)

Fuchs, D. Reading and perceptual motor performance: Can we strengthen them simultaneously? *The Journal of Special Education*, 1979, 13, 265-273.

Gavin, R.T. The relationship between perceptual-motor training and perceptual-motor status and school achievement (Doctoral dissertation, Rutgers University, The State University of New Jersey, 1976). *Dissertation Abstracts International*, 1977, 37, 7682A. (University Microfilms No. 77-13-264)

Gentry, L.A. A clinical method in classroom success - - kinesthetic teaching. *The Reading Teacher*, 1974, 28, 298-300.

Gibbs, V., & Proctor, S. Reading together: An experiment with the neurological-impress method. *Contemporary Education*, 1977, 48, 156-157.

Gillingham, A., & Stillman, B.W. *Remedial training for children with specific disability in reading, spelling and penmanship.* Parts I & II. New York: Anna Gillingham and Bessie W. Stillman, 1946.

Glass, G. U., & Stanley, J.C. *Statistical methods in education and psychology.* Englewood Cliffs, N.J.: Prentice-Hall, 1970.

Gredler, G.R. Learning disabilities and reading disorders: A current assessment. *Psychology in the Schools,* 1978, 15, 226-238.

Hallahan, D.P., & Cruickshank, W.M. *Psycho-educational foundations of learning disabilities.* Engelwood Cliffs, N.J.: Prentice-Hall, 1973.

Halliwell, J.W. & Solan, H.A. The effects of a supplement perceptual training program on reading achievement. *Exceptional Children*, 1972, 38, 613-621.

Harris, A.J. *How to increase reading ability* (5th ed,) New York: David McKay Company, 1970.

Harris, A.J. A reaction to Valtin's "Dyslexia: Deficit in reading or deficit in research?" *Reading Research Quarterly*, 1978-1979, 14, 222-225.

Harris, A.J. Ten years of progress in remedial reading. *Journal of Reading*, 1977, 21, 29-35.

Heckelman, R.G. A neurological-impress method of remedial-reading instruction. *Academic Therapy*, 1969, 4, 277-282.

Hollingsworth, P.M. An experimental approach to the impress method of teaching reading. *The Reading Teacher*, 1978, 31, 624-626.

Jansson, D.R., & Schillereff, T. Reinforcing remedial readers through art activities. *The Reading Teacher*, 1980, 33, 548-551.

Kampwirth, T.J. Not just another ficsh story: A response to Barbe, Swassing and Milone. *Academic Therapy*, 1981, 16, 267-269.

Kampwirth, T.J. & Bates, M. Modality preference and teaching method: A review of the research. *Academic Therapy*, 1980, 15, 597-605.

Kephart, N.C. *The slow learner in the classroom.* Columbus, Ohio: Charles E. Merrill Books, 1960.

Kirk, S.A., & Kirk, W.D. *Psycholinguistic learning disabilities: Diagnosis and remediation.* Chicago: University of Illinois Press, 1971.

Kline C.L. Developmental dyslexia in adolescents: The emotional carnage. *Bulletin of the Orton Society*, 1978, 28, 160-174.

Kline, C.L. Orton-Gillingham methodology: Where have all of the researchers gone? *Bulletin of the Orton Society*, 1977, 27, 82-87.

Kline, C.L. & Kline, C.L. Follow-up study of 216 dyslexic children. *Bulletin of the Orton Society*, 1975, 25, 127-144.

Koepsel, E.O. A comparison of teaching reading to educationally handicapped childrens Fernald's VAKT method, Blaus' AKT method, and existing methods (Doctoral Dissertation, University of Northern Colorado, 1974.) *Dissertation Abstracts International*, 1975, 35, 7157A. (University Microfilms No. 75-11-097)

Lacey, T.P. A program to identify and remediate learning disabled children with perceptual-motor impairments at the intermediate grade levels (Doctoral dissertation, University of Utah, 1975.) *Dissertation Abstracts International*, 1975, 36, 3386A. University Microfilms No. 75-28-869)

Langford, K., Slade, K. & Barnett, A. An examination of impress techniques in remedial reading. *Academic Therapy*, 1974, 9, 309-319.

Leviton, H.S. Person or machine in remedial reading? *Academic Therapy*, 1976, 11, 455-459.

Lorenx, L. & Vockell, E. Using the neurological impress method with learning disabled readers. *Journal of Learning Disabilities*, 1979, **12**, 67-69.

Lovenspiel, M.J. A study of the relationships between perceptual-motor behaviors and: achievement in reading; achievement in mathematics; classroom behavior; academic self-concept; and academic motivation for first and third grade boys and girls (Doctoral Dissertation, Oregon State University, 1975.) *Dissertation Abstracts International*, 1975, 36, 818A. (University Microfilms No. 75-16-814)

Masland, R.L. Subgroups in dyslexia: Issues of definition. *Bulletin of the Orton Society*, 1979, 29, 23-30.

Meyers, M.C. The significance of learning modalities, modes of instruction, and verbal feedback for word recognition of learning disabled students (Doctoral dissertation, University of South Florida, 1977. *Dissertation Abstracts International*, 1977, 38, 4098A. (University Microfilms No. 77-28-164)

Miccinati, J. The Fernald technique: Modifications increase the probability of success. *Journal of Learning Disabilities*, 1979, 12, 6-9.

Miller, S.R. & Sabatino, D.A. Evaluating the instructional effectiveness of supplemental special education materials. *Exceptional Children*, 1977, 43, 457-461.

Money, J. *The Disabled Reader*, Baltimore: The Johns Hopkins Press, 1966.

Morrissey, P.J. Pre-academic predictors of success in a multisensory reading program (Doctoral dissertation, University of San Francisco, 1979.) *Dissertation Abstracts International*, 1980, 41, 202A. (University Microfilms No. 80-12-134)

Myers, C.A. Reviewing the literature on Fernald's technique of remedial reading. *The Reading Teacher*, 1977, 31, 614-619.

Orton, S.T. *"Word blindness" in school children and other papers on strephosymbolia*. Pomfret, Conn.: The Orton Society, 1966.

Rawson, M.B. *Developmental language disability: Adult accomplishments of dyslexic boys.* Baltimore: The Johns Hopkins Press, 1978.

Richards, J. It's all right if kids can't read. *Journal of Learning Disabilities*, 1981, 14, 62-67.

Rupley, W.H. & Blair, T.R. Remedial reading instruction. *The Reading Teacher*, 1977, 30, 708-711.

Ruppert, E.T. The effect of the synthetic-multisensory method of language instruction upon psycholinguistic abilities and reading achievement (Doctoral dissertation, The American University, 1976.) *Dissertation Abstracts International*, 1976, 37, 920A. (University Microfilms No. 76-18-223)

Rydack, D. A "sweep" procedure for reading improvement. *Reading Improvement*, 1976, 13, 101-102.

Satz, P., Friel, J. & Goebel, R.A. Some predictive antecedents of specific reading disability: A three year follow-up. *Bulleting of the Orton Society.* 1975, 25, 91-110.

Schweizer, I.T. Orton revisited. *Reading Teacher*, 1974, 28, 295-297.

Sears, C.J. The tactilely defensive child. *Academic Therapy*, 1981, 16, 563-569.

Shankweiler, D., & Liberman, I.Y. Reading behavior in dyslexia: Is there a distinctive pattern? *Bulletin of the Orton Society*, 1978, 28, 114-123.

Shore, B. & Riegel, P. Teaching reading to the child with perceptual deficits. *Academic Therapy*, 1978, 13, 337-343.

Solem, M.A.R. A comparative study of five alternative reading programs and the learning profiles of disabled readers (Doctoral dissertation, University of South Dakota, 1976.) *Dissertation Abstracts International*, 2979, 39, 5313A-5314A. (University Microfilms No. 79-04-925)

Spalding, R.B., & Spalding, W.T. *The writing road to reading* (2nd revised edition) New York: William Morow & Company, 1969.

St. John, P.A.W. Effects of a remedial art program for visuo-spatial-motor skills on drawings by neurologically impaired children: A multicase study (Doctoral dissertation, Columbia University Teachers College, 1978.) *Dissertation Abstracts International*, 1979, 39, 5883A. (University Microfilms No. 79-09-025)

Sydnor, C.A. The relationship between reading achievement and academic achievement for program graduates of the diagnostic and remedial reading program of the Richmond School (Doctoral dissertation, University of Virginia, 1976.) *Dissertation Abstracts International*, 1977, 37, 4149A. (University Microfilms No. 77-00-185)

Tallal, P. Language and reading: Some perceptual prerequisites. *Bulletin of the Orton Society*, 1980, 30, 170-178.

Taylor, E.M.W. The effect of perceptual training in the classroom (Doctoral dissertation, Wayne State University, 1976.) *Dissertation Abstracts International*, 1977, 37, 6938A. (University Microfilms No. 77-90-457)

Valett, R. *Dyslexia: A neuropsychological approach to educating children with severe reading disorders*. Belmont, California: Fearon Pitman Publishers, 1980.

Valett, R. Dyslexia: Deficit in reading or deficit in research? *Reading Research Quarterly*, 1978-1979, 14, 202-221.

Waites, L. *Specific developmental dyslexia and related language disabilities*. Dallas, Texas Scottish Rite Hospital for Crippled Children, 1969.

Warren, L.M. Efficacy of Fernald and Gillingham multi-sensory reading approaches: A comparative study and investigation of related variable (Doctoral dissertation, The University of Alabama, 1977.) *Dissertation Abstracts International*, 1978, 39, 2189A. (University Microfilms No. 78-18-908)

Witelson, S.F. Developmental dyslexia: Two right hemispheres and none left. *Science*, 1977, 3, 309-311.

Witman, C.C, & Riley, J.D. Colored chalk and messy fingers: A kinesthetic-tactile approach to reading, *The Reading Teacher*, 1978, 31, 620-623.

PRELIMINARY EVALUATION

SUB — TESTS

MODALITY	LEARNING PROCESS	SUB TEST
Visual Processing	Visual Sequencing	WISC-R Picture Arrangement
	Visual Memory	Bender - Gestalt
	Visual Abstraction	WISC-R Picture Completion
	Visual Discrimination	Frostig
Auditory Processing	Auditory Sequencing	WISC-R Digit Span
	Auditory Memory	Detroit (DTLA) Unrelated Words
	Auditory Abstraction	WISC-R Comprehension
	Auditory Discrimination	Wepman - Auditory Discrimination
Verbal Processing	Verbal Production	WISC-R Vocabulary
	Verbal Response	WISC-R Information
Kinesthetic Processing	Kinesthetic Perception	WISC-R Mazes
	Kinesthetic Coordination	WISC-R Object Assembly
	Kinesthetic Learning	WISC-R Coding
Abstract Processing	Integration	WISC-R Similarities
	Non Verbal Concept Formation	WISC-R Block Design
	Concentration	WISC-R Arithmetic

VERIFICATION

SUB—TESTS

MODALITY	LEARNING PROCESS	SUB TEST
Visual Processing	Visual Sequencing	ITPA Visual Sequential Memory
	Visual Memory	Detroit (DTLA) Memory for Design
	Visual Abstraction	Detroit (DTLA) Pictorial Absurdities
	Visual Discrimination	Frostig
Auditory Processing	Auditory Sequencing	Detroit (DTLA) Related Words
	Auditory Memory	Wepman Auditory Memory
	Auditory Abstraction	Detroit (DTLA) Similarities & Differences
	Auditory Discrimination	ITPA Auditory Closure
Verbal Processing	Verbal Production	Peabody Vocabulary
	Verbal Response	Gray Oral Reading
Kinesthetic Processing	Kinesthetic Perception	ITPA Visual Motor Association
	Kinesthetic Coordination	Bender - Gestalt
	Kinesthetic Learning	ITPA Manual Expression
Abstract Processing	Integrative Processing	Detroit (DTLA) Pictorial Similarities
	NonVerbal Concept Formation	Leiter Non Verbal
	Concentration	Detroit (DTLA) Attention Span for Unrelated Words